Abh

River Valley to Silicon Valley
Story of three generations of an
Indian family

Abhay K.

River Valley to Silicon Valley

Story of three generations of an Indian family

BOOKWELL

River Valley to Silicon Valley
by
Abhay K.

Copyright © Abhay Kumar, 2007

ISBN: 81-89640-39-9

First Published in India in 2007 by:

BOOKWELL

Sales Office

24/4800, Ansari Road,
Darya Ganj,
New Delhi-110002, India
Ph: 91-11-23268786

Head Office:

2/72, Nirankari Colony,
Delhi-110009, India
Ph: 91-11-27251283
Fax: 91-11-23281315

E-mail: bkwell@nde.vsnl.net.in
bookwell@vsnl.net

The Cover page is a part of a painting by Yang Jian Feng

Computer Typesetting by:
Shubham Computer, Delhi

Printed at D.K. Fine Art Press P. Ltd., Delhi-110052

FOR MY GREAT FATHER
who inspired me
the way he lived till the end

And for the new generation of youth in
India who are ready to make a difference

Contents

FOREWORD

This is a sincere, simple and readable account of Abhay Kumar's journey from the banks of the river Paimar to the portals of the Foreign Service Institute in New Delhi. This is a story many young Indians could relate to, those with rural and educationally disadvantaged backgrounds successfully transforming their personal lives and prospects by availing of the opportunities that India's democratic system and its recent economic growth provide. In its own way, the book is a positive commentary on the process of change in Indian society, on the scope for self-advancement even to the point of becoming a part of the country's elite through education and competition that now exists. The human content of the narrative will also touch many chords in the readers. The childhood memories of stories told by a grandmother, the venturing out from the family nest in rural India to an urban environment in search for better opportunities in life, and the presence of the father on the emotional landscape of an Indian boy. This is not a complicated book; it is an unpretentious and honest narrative of someone who wants to tell his tale and connect it to a rising India.

K.Sibal
Moscow,
17 April 2007
Ambassador of India
to the Russian Federation

INTRODUCTION

India is an enigma wrapped in several layers. It opens as much as one tries to get into its depth.

India is known to the world since the time of the Greek Historian Herodotus who believed that gold-digging ants existed in India. India since then has always been a blend of fact and fantasy for the outside world. Megesthenes, the Greek envoy to the court of the great Indian emperor Chandragupta Maurya (320-297 BC) wrote a firsthand account of India in which he painted an idyllic picture of life in India. In the medieval times Arab travelers Al Beruni and Ibn Batuta wrote the greatest accounts of India. Despite these accounts by great travelers and scholars the myth and legend of India continued in absence of concrete information about this vast and diverse land.

The mysterious veil that covered India was lifted with the opening of the sea route to India from Europe and the arrival of the traders. These traders encountered a civilization with such a great diversity that they found it difficult to grasp the essence of India. The legend of India's enormous wealth that had brought them here was real but they found a society ridden with great complexities of multiple castes, religions and languages and formed their own assumptions and prejudices over a course of time about India.

Since the time of the ancient Greeks to modern day, a variety of assumptions and prejudices about India have persisted in the mind of the outsiders. This is strange that the same assumptions and prejudices have lasted over two millennia.

'River Valley to Silicon Valley' is an endeavor to go into the depth of the enigma that is India through a story spanning over three generations of an Indian family. India over this time span has transformed itself from a slow growing backward British colony into a successful and modern secular democracy. Today India is a dynamic economy with one of the fastest economic growth rates in the world. It has emerged as a global economic power as the world's third largest economy in terms of purchasing power parity. The economic transformation of India has been miraculous in the last few decades. The percentage share of agriculture in the total Gross Domestic Product (GDP) of the country has slid below twenty percent while the percentage share of services amounts to more than fifty percent of its GDP.

India is now the focus of the global media attention. Its contributions especially in the Information Technology (IT) sector accompanied with its fast economic growth rate have brought India to the centre stage of global media attention. India's fast rise in the IT sector has been noted by the world to such an extent that there is a threat of extreme stereotyping an Indian as a computer whiz kid or a software engineer. India's world renowned success in the IT sector has infused positive energies in Indians and now this success story is being repeated in other areas including some more noteworthy ones like pharmaceutical, steel, space, and automobile industries.

Outsiders often think these changes to be superficial as millions of Indians still live below the poverty line; almost half of its children grow up malnourished and tensions persist in many forms and shapes in the society throughout the length and breadth of the country with a constant fear of rise of insurgency, outbreak of a riot etc. But India has undergone through some real and irreversible changes on the path of becoming a modern secular democracy with a fast growing dynamic economy.

'River Valley to Silicon Valley' is an account of such gradual and persistent changes that India has undergone in the past few decades. The greatness and beauty of India is in its diversity where grandpa in the River valley and grandson in the Silicon Valley coexist side by side. One at ease with grazing cows and growing vegetables in the green fields by the river and with his 'river-valley civilization life style' in the 'agricultural age' as he has been there since centuries, since the very beginning of mankind's arrival while the other at ease with a new era of 'information age' where space and time hardly matter, jobs are available across the globe and business is conducted 24X7 online.

The River Valley

Life's but a walking shadow,
A poor player
That struts and frets his hour on the stage
And then is heard no more
It's a tale told by an idiot
Full of sound and fury
Signifying nothing

Macbeth, William Shakespeare

My grandfather was a local wrestler. He started each morning by putting a handful of soil on his body to strengthen it a little before wrestling with at least ten other wrestlers from the neighbouring villages. He lived as the early humans did in the beginning of the river valley civilizations like the Nile, the Mesopotamia or the Indus. He cultivated grains and vegetables and reared animals for a livelihood on the banks of the river *Paimar*[1] while my grandma looked after the household chores, cooked food. Besides that she also worked in the fields along with my grandfather. My grandma was beautiful woman with a large heart. They had many children but out of them only four boys and three girls survived.

My father was the eldest among the seven boys and girls. He took the family responsibilities early, stepping into his father's shoes when he was still a seven year old child. He accompanied his father to the river bank everyday. He graze cows and worked in the fields along with his father, but his heart lied somewhere else. One day he broke the centuries old family tradition of cow grazing and farming by going to a school. Each day he walked to the school and back home for ten miles. He spent his mornings and evenings teaching his

---

[1]   A small river in the district of Nalanda in the state of Bihar in East India, dries up in summer

younger brothers, sisters and cousins how to read and write and helping his mother to feed the cattle. My grandpa's family was a large joint family comprising of his parents and the family of his two brothers.

Those days India had just become independent and the green revolution was still two decades away. Such a large family had barely enough to eat. They survived on *Marua*[2]. It easily grew in the less-fertile lands with little water available for irrigation in the dry season. The Paimar was like any other Indian river. It had mood swings, flooding the lands and villages located on its banks in the rainy *monsoon*[3] season and drying up in the hot Indian tropical summer. Irrigation facilities were very little developed. For irrigation that time there was only *latha-Kuri*[4] in the village and it was only functional when there was sufficient water flow in the river Paimar. *Persian*

---

[2]   A coarse food grain
[3]   A seasonal reversal of winds that causes rainfall in most part of India from July to early October
[4]   A tradition equipment operated manually used in the Indian villages for irrigation

Wheels[5] were more advanced means of irrigation but they were expensive to buy at the first instance. They were available in the more prosperous villages but my grandpa's family could not afford such convenience yet. Canals were also being planned by the district irrigation department but they had not been dug yet.

My father grew up in such social and economic circumstances. He got whatever education he could manage to get, apart from working in the fields with his father, rearing animals and taking care of his younger brothers, sisters and cousins. He always stood first in his class despite putting such hard work in the fields and performing home chores. The teachers at the school always praised his hard work and determination. He passed his *Matriculation*[6] exam earning a second *division*[7]. Such a high score was a matter of envy for the

---

[5] Animal driven large water wheel, turned by the action of a stream against its floats, and carrying at its circumference buckets, by which water is raised and discharged into a trough; used in Arabia, China, and elsewhere for irrigating land; a Persian wheel.

[6] An examination after the tenth class

[7] Score between 45-60 out of 100

students of many villages who only dreamed to somehow pass the matriculation exam. After passing matriculation he took admission in a college for an Intermediate course but he could not study there for long, as a large family had its own priorities, to feed the children first and then if some money could be spared then that could support my father's higher studies.

As soon as it became clear that my father could not study any further because of the financial problems, our family came to the conclusion that it was the time for him to get married. My grandfather was a well known wrestler in many neighbouring villages and when he announced that his eldest son would get married soon, it became a matter of discussion and interest in several surrounding villages. Everybody put one's mind to work to think of a suitable girl for my father.

Mahtoji from the *Rehua*[8] village, about four-five kilometres away from my grandpa's village, was one of the most influential people in many surrounding villages. Mahtoji was known for his wit and wisdom in the far off villages. He took a keen interest in my

---

[8]   The native village of my mother, named after a fish

grandpa's will to find a suitable girl for my father. Mahtoji wasted no time and set his journey along the banks of the river Paimar and didn't stop until he reached my grandpa home in *Bhattubigha*[9]. He was more than impressed to see my father, a young handsome matriculate man. He saw in him a man full of courage and determination to change things for better and wasted no time in inviting my grandpa to his native village *Rehua* to see his eldest daughter on an auspicious day. My grandpa was attracted to the intellect and wit of Mahtoji. This was a relationship between two families, one reputed for wrestling and the other for the intellect.

My grandpa visited *Rehua* to see Mahtoji's eldest daughter on an auspicious day. She came out in a green sari holding a pot full of water with her both hands. He asked her to tell the names of her grandfathers and grandmothers, what she could cook and their recipes, counting of the numerals and basic sums of algebra. She answered most of them to my grandfather's satisfaction. Then she was asked to walk

---

[9]   A small village named after my great grandpa Shri Bhattu Singh

around a little so that my grandfather could check whether she could walk properly or not. After half and hour of exchange of ideas among themselves my grandfather along with his other relatives who were also present on the occasion reached the conclusion that Mahtoji's eldest daughter was indeed a suitable girl for my father and the two families could become relatives. A marriage deal was reached over a Hercules bicycle along with a hundred rupees as dowry to my father in his marriage with my mother.

My mother's family was better off socially and economically than my father's family although she too had a large family with five brothers and three sisters. Her father was a *Mahto*[10] that meant that he was a village leader and had more land and cattle than others in his native village and the adjoining villages. He also owned a bullock cart and that was a very prestigious thing to own that time. Mahtoji read *Ramayana*[11] with a great flair in those times when only a few among the villagers

---

[10] Local village chief
[11] Great Indian epic about a prince Rama, his wife Sita and the abductor of Sita ,Ravana

could read and write. Even today an Indian possessing a copy of Ramayana who has the ability to recite it by heart is revered in the Indian villages.

Finally the marriage took place in the dawn, on an auspicious day in the month of *baishakh*[12]. This marriage was a great event for both the families as their eldest son and daughter was getting married that day and after all that was the first marriage in their families in a generation's time. People came to attend the marriage ceremony from the distant villages in many bullock carts; it was a grand ceremony. After marriage, my mother came to a new home that was not as rich as her *naihar*[13]. It was not more than a few straw hutments located on the banks of the river Paimar that could be blow away by the wind easily during a storm. Her *sasural*[14] did not even have a copy of the sacred Ramayana. She had come from a home that was always full of *dudh-ghee*[15] and there was never a shortage of food grains or fresh vegetables. Her new home was

---

[12] The second month of the Hindu Saka Samvat (calendar)

[13] Mother's ancestral home

[14] The home of the in laws

[15] Milk and clarified butter

nothing but mud walls and straw roof and faced persistent scarcities of food and clean water. Nevertheless she was happy and adapted herself rather well after the initial difficulties.

She liked the flow of river *Paimar* where she washed her clothes and took baths. The River offered her something new, something she had not had before, perhaps freedom to be on her own. With cool and fresh flow of life-giving water of the river Paimar she had found her own flow, her destiny like my father she too wanted to study further and to become a teacher but due to marriage she had to leave her own plans and dedicate her all love and energy to her new family, the family she was married into. She cooked food for the whole extended family, even though sometimes she felt it was too big to manage, brought up all the children as her own and kept the whole family glued together with her overflowing love and sheer hard work.

My father's desires were smothered in want of money but his dreams never died. Even after his marriage he continued to look for opportunities to improve his knowledge and find a suitable job. He somehow got the inspiration to become an *overseer*[16], perhaps from looking at the overseers who came to inspect the newly built canals for irrigation near the village. He applied through one of these overseers into a Polytechnic Institute for admission. Happily he was invited to join the course in that institute. He needed just Rupees 500 *(~US$100)*[17] for the admission· in the polytechnic institute but he could not afford it, the whole family together could not afford it. In those days it was a large sum of money and the family had hardly any extra money to spend on education when it could barely meet its food necessities. He thought of borrowing this sum from his father-in-law but he was against my father going away to a distant town to study polytechnic and refused to lend any money.

My father had hardly any choice but to be content with working in the fields, growing *Marua* and vegetables. Nevertheless at the same time he started teaching the children from the other nearby villages and soon joined the teacher training program offered by the State

---

[16]   A junior civil engineer below the rank of executive engineer

[17]   By rupee –dollar exchange rate those days

government. After successfully completing the training program, he was formally appointed as a teacher in a *Village Primary School*[18] not very far away from his native village. From there onwards he continued teaching children for more than three decades.

My parents had lost three children one after the other because of the lack of the medical facilities and the absence of the connectivity of the village to any nearby town where such facilities were easily available. The fourth child survived with the grace of God and brought a new hope to the whole family. My parents were worried for the survival of their only living child. They wanted to move to a new place as soon as possible that at least had a connecting road to a nearby town along with the bus service. They did find such a place, their *El Dorado*, but it had little but a few straw hutments. My father was initially disappointed but he had no choice but to settle at this new place, the place that, he thought, had myriad possibilities. He bought a little piece of land there and started building a house slowly with money from his savings. He put the foundations

---

[18]   From class one to class five

of a new house by laying bricks himself. The inhabitants of other straw hutments did not take it very kindly as they saw the laying of bricks as an assault on the dignity of their straw hutments. The next morning when my father came to the building site he found his bricks had disappeared overnight. He was disappointed with such an attitude of the other villagers towards a new settler. Nevertheless he started all over again; he laid the foundations all over again and in the evening put a person on the site to guard over the night. In the next two decades slowly and gradually with his savings he built a beautiful concrete house with a grand courtyard and a little garden in the front of the house. He taught the children of the villagers free of cost and motivated them to educate their children even if it meant eating only one meal a day.

Fortunately, my elder brother survived despite all the odds. Now my father's salary could buy my elder brother necessary medicines and nutritious fruits. He grew up to be a healthy kid.

I was born after five years of the birth of my brother. My mother often tells me that I was born after she had offered many prayers to the local village deities. And as a part of ritual these deities must be offered a lock of my hair one day. I must have my head shaved one fine morning on the banks of the Paimar to fulfil the wishes of my mother, the village deity, priest and my relatives.

A year or two after my birth my parents moved to a new village, *Chhabilapur*[19] while our house was still being built. The new village was located beside a main road connecting the town of *Rajgir*[20] with the state capital *Patna*[21]. A canal flowed in the north of the village. It had a bus station where villagers gathered during the day to commute to the nearby towns. Along with the other village children I too was amazed by the noise a motor vehicle running on the road made and we all ran out towards the road to see a bus. My new village *Chhabilapur* was interesting but it had no comparison with my ancestral village *Bhattubigha*.

---

[19] Means a place with beauty and colours

[20] A beautiful town surrounded by the hills, Rajgir was the ancient capital of the Magadh empire

[21] Earlier known as Patliputra, now the capital of the state of Bihar in Eastern India

When I turned seven I started going to my grandpa's house with my elder brother to visit our grandpa, grandma, uncles and aunties, and our cousins. We often brought *datuns*[22] and *mitha*[23] from there. We had to cross the river Paimar after an hour's walk from my new home to reach there. I loved going there to meet my grandma, eat guavas and swim in the river Paimar. She told me endless stories at night while I slept in her arms clinging to her soft & loose skin.

Whenever I arrived at my grandma's home she would take me in her arms and kiss me and then take me to the small orchard in front of our house to get me fresh guavas from the tree. I loved plucking and eating guavas with my grandma in the orchard. It was our little paradise, the paradise where the Sun eternally shined and the fresh whiff of wind never stopped blowing. Then we went to the field and she got me sweet sugarcane to chew. I always insisted that the sugarcane be cut into pieces for me because I could not eat the whole

---

[22] Mouth brushes made from either Neem or Babool plants

[23] A product prepared in the villages after raw sugarcane juice is heated for a long time

sugarcane on my own. It required some skills that only grown ups possessed, that I had not acquired yet.

At night she told me stories until I fell asleep in her arms. She put oil in my hair, combed it and put *kajal*[24] on my forehead to save me from evil eyes. I loved bathing in the Paimar but grandma did not allow me to bathe in the river because she feared I could catch cold and fever.

'Now I can say that I had some of the most blissful days on the earth playing with other village kids, just running carefree in the mango grooves outside my home, plucking *guavas* and *Bers*[25] along the banks of the Paimar. I have never felt that bliss again since I left the banks of the Paimar for my new home and then kept on moving from village to town and from town to city and mega city.'

Parting from my grandma was the most painful thing for me as there was no other bliss than to drowse off and to fall asleep in

---

[24] Black cosmetic product made by mixing shoot and oil, used as eye liner and villagers believe that it keeps the evil away

[25] Plums

her soft sweet arms listening to her stories at night. I wanted her to come to my new home and stay with me but Grandpa would not let her come with me. I always returned home a little lost and with many good stories that grandma told me.

Those days as a little kid those days I wondered about the continuous noise all the time coming out from the trees and the ponds. I thought it must be permanent background sound of the nature. Later I realized my misunderstanding when I visited the town for the first time. The noise of buses, trucks, machines and the market place filled my ears. I discovered that the constant noise in the village came from the trees and the ponds and the cicadas, grasshoppers and the frogs that inhabited them.

I liked my new home but not as much as I liked my grandpa's home. I often used to go to the neighbours' homes to play where there used to be many kids. We played together everyday till t my father came looking for me to take me home to study. Some kids did not like me because my father was a school teacher and he did not let other kids play games like *kancha*[26] and *gulli- danda*[27] because they could prove to be harmful at times.

The first school I attended was the school my father had started for the village kids as there was no school in the village. The school had two rooms and a veranda where we sang the morning prayers. The two rooms accommodated five classes from the first to fifth standards. We carried *'boras'*[28] from our home as we sat on the earthen ground, sometimes wet in the rainy reason due to water trickling from the old dilapidated tiled roof. On Saturday afternoons, we washed the floor of the two rooms and the veranda with *'gobar'*[29].The school had no toilet. Many *Ber* trees were behind the school building where we went for the numbers "1" and "2". These were the vital numbers for the nature's calls, as we were not allowed to say the actual Hindi words for these activities. The number 'One' stood for a very

---

26 Small solid balls made of glass and used by children for playing

27 A game played in the villages of India in which a small stick is hit by a long one, dangerous if played in a crowded place

28 Bags made of plastic or jute and is used for sitting if spread on the floor

29 Cow dung

small break while the number 'Two' for a little longer one than the number one. A small rivulet flowed not very far from the school building, where we used to go sometimes to relieve ourselves or to just wonder about when the classes became too heavy for us.

The school ran for just two years and then got closed due to financial problems as the students could not pay their monthly fees. I moved to a new school in a nearby village where I was admitted in the third standard in the primary school. Shri *Jagdish* was a teacher who passed through my village everyday en route to a nearby village where my new school was located. My father had requested him to take me along with him to the school while going to the school and bring me home while returning from the school to his village. He was not only a good teacher but a poet too. He often read his poems to me on the way to the school and back home. Though I was only eight that time I understood and liked his poems as they were lyrical and focused on the local developmental issues, the progress of our society and the nation.

I went to that school for a year and passed the fourth standard. Then I had to change this school again for a government middle school where students of fifth to eight standard studied. The middle school was located along a canal in the middle of the two villages. The morning here started with prayers and afterwards classes went on till one o' clock in the afternoon. During the lunch break students played cricket and rode bicycles in the playground located in front of the school. They performed some dare-devil tricks to impress the school girls. I ate peanuts and ice-cream in lunch as I always had heavy breakfast in the morning and when I set out for school my mother fed me again. Classes ended at five and I walked back home with the other children from my village. In the midway we sat under a big banyan tree beside a big pond to rest for a while. People said ghosts lived on that tree but there was nothing to be scared of as other children always accompanied me but when sometimes I travelled alone I ran with full force until I got far away from that banyan tree and reached the main road.

Though I liked the middle school a lot I wanted to study in a town school. I had heard that schools in the town were much better and helped students to prepare for the competitive entrance exams for better schools in the State. Whenever I asked my parents to allow me to go to the nearby town to study they told me that I was too young to live on my own away from them. At that time *Shri Dinanath*, a teacher, who had taught me earlier in my father's school came to my rescue. After the school started by father had got closed due to financial problems he had gone to the nearby town Rajgir. He taught in one of the schools there. When he came to visit my parents I asked him if he could take me along to the town and get me admitted there. He kindly agreed and both of us convinced my parents not to worry as he promised to take care of me in the school hostel. My parents finally agreed to let me go after a long deliberation on this matter.

2

From the Paimar to the Ganges

The tide rises, the tide falls,
The twilight darkens, the curlew calls;
Along the sea-sands damp and brown
The traveller hastens toward the town,
 And the tide rises, the tide falls.

-Henry Wadsworth Longfellow

I was very happy to study in the new school nevertheless it was unbearable for me to stay away from my mother. When I spent my first night away from home I silently sobbed for the whole night wanting all the time to run away to my mother at the first sight of the dawn but with the dawn my mind suddenly remembered how hard I had tried to get my parent's concurrence to let me go to a town school. I was sure that my parents missed me too but they had made this hard decision for me. In the new school-hostel rules were very strict and it was impossible to escape from this self-created prison. My father came to see me every week but I saw my mother only once a month when I was allowed to go home just for a day. I could not stay in this school for long. In a short time I found out that it was not one of the best schools in the town to prepare myself for the competitive exams to enter some of the best schools in our state *Bihar*[1] viz. *Navodaya, Neterhat or Sainik* Schools. The state government provided quality education free of cost in these schools and paid for all other expenses. These schools were very popular among the people of our state 'Bihar' for providing the best education in the state. They

---

[1]   A state in east India, named after Viharas (Buddhist monasteries) has one of the lowest level of literacy and large number of people living below poverty line

had very limited intake each year and the competition to get into them was very tough.

Soon I decided to join another school which had a better reputation in preparing students for the competitive exams for admission in these popular schools. I was admitted into sixth standard in *Gyan Niketan*. I worked hard and completed two classes in one year jumping into eighth standard the next year along with preparing for the competitive exams. I liked Gyan Niketan a lot and I spent the next eighteen months there. This school had a very competitive ambience and a number of very hard working students. Girls were pretty and boys had to prove themselves to attract their attention. The day here began at four in the morning with everybody waking up with the sound of the loudly ringing bell. I hated getting up that early in the morning. I was sure none among my schoolmates really liked it getting up at four in the morning when one had the best sleep except those grown-up teachers who, I was sure, could not sleep well at night. With the sound of the bell everyone rushed to the big veranda for the prayer. Basically the prayer was meant to break our drowsiness. Students just lazily tried to croak out some sounds out of their throats in place of any meaningful prayer. I could always hear some of the students cursing the teachers for not letting them sleep a little longer in the early morning when they probably had their best sleep. The *laltens*[2] were lit and we sat in circles on the cold and hard *'chowkis'*[3] to read loudly. I was sure the neighbouring homes around the school had tough time too as more than a hundred children reading loudly together generated considerable noise. A number of teachers kept watch of the students. Each one of us was monitored by them carefully. They checked if anyone was sleeping or drowsing off. These acts invited quick punishment, either a tight slap on the cheeks or caning on the back.

After an hour of loud recitals there was another bell and students were herded in a queue. Counting began in the queue to check whether anyone was missing or not. The missing ones were located and punished, as there were always a few who went on missing. The missing students were often found to be

[2]   Lanterns using kerosene as fuel spreading dim light
[3]   Hard wooden bed

sleeping in the toilet or under the *Chowkis* and brought to join the queue after suitable punishment. Soon the queue was turned into a marching band of soldiers and we all proceeded to relieve ourselves in the open in a secluded corner in the foothills of *Rajgir*[4] where ample water flowed in the *'nalas'*[5] to wash our bottoms. After we relieved ourselves we queued up again and proceeded to the *'Kund'*[6] to bathe ourselves. We marched back to the school hostel by eight o' clock in the morning and had *'Chana'*[7] soaked overnight in water and *'Gur*[8]*'* for the breakfast.

After a quick breakfast we queued up again at 9 a.m. for a morning prayer and half an hour session of physical exercises (PT). The prayer used to be different this time, a bit more enthusiastic, a bit livelier than the early Morning Prayer. I had introduced the idea of reading the headlines from a local newspaper to the students after the prayer and I loved doing it after the boring PT everyday. Classes started

---

[4] The ancient capital of the Magadh empire
[5] Drains
[6] Warm water springs
[7] Grams
[8] Raw sugar

at 10 a.m. in the morning and stopped only at 1 p.m. in the afternoon for the lunch break for an hour.

As soon as the bell rang we all ran to get our plates from our rooms that we usually kept below the bed, sometimes even inside the box safely locked ensuring that they were not stolen or used by someone else. The rush continued to get ahead in the queue for the lunch. We were anywhere between hundred to hundred fifty students in the school hostel and just getting ahead in the queue really mattered a lot because if one could get ahead in the queue then one could steal some time for playing carom, lido, ring ball or badminton during the lunch break. Lunch generally consisted of cooked rice, *dal*[9], *bhujia*[10], or *subji*.[11] Potato used to be the usual ingredient of *subji*. Green vegetables were rare commodities. We had major complaints against the *dal* that was served to us in the hostel mess. It was generally thin and runny. Even some small uprisings were organized by a few more courageous among us in the hostel around the burning issue of

---

[9]   A curry dish made out of pulses
[10]   Potatoes fried in oil
[11]   Cooked vegetables

thin and runny *dal* before the hostel warden but most of them were brutally suppressed by the Principal of the school with little improvements.

Time passed by fast and there came a time when school authorities decided to shift the school to a new location far away from the old location and a little away from the main town of Rajgir. The new location was not very safe because of the occurrence of a few incidents of kidnapping of the school children from that area for a ransom. I badly wanted to be with my mother at home and I was looking forward for an excuse to live with my mother for a while. I left this school with the excuse that I might get kidnapped in the new location as it was a little away from the main town.

I wanted to come home but my father had some other plans for me. My elder brother that time lived in *Biharshariff*[12] renting a room. He studied in Intermediate Science (I.Sc.) course in Nalanda College. My father asked me to live with him for a while and try out a new school there. I went there with a heavy heart as I wanted to be with my mother. The new place

---

[12] The district headquarter of Nalanda district, a religious site as well

turned out to be very boring and suffocating for me as I was continuously advised by my elder brother "what to do, what not to do". I needed my space and badly wanted to be with my mother so after spending a few months with my brother I returned home to live with my parents.

After getting finally back to home I took admission in *Andhabas*[13] High School. It was located fifteen minutes bicycle ride from my village. I asked my father for a new bicycle but he suggested that I buy an old one or get repaired the one he had got as gift from his in-laws in marriage, rotting in the store room since many years. Finally I got his Hercules bicycle repaired and used it for a year.

To live at home with my mother after such a long time was such a luxury. I really enjoyed it. In the new school I quickly found a few friends. The school building was a linear whitewashed building with a huge playground in the front. It was school for the minority community run and managed by the state Government. We sang in the morning *'Sare Jahan Se Achha Hindostan Hamara*[14]' by the great

---

[13]   It is not clear what does the name mean
[14]   Our India is better than the rest of the world

poet *Iqbal*[15] and we had 'Friday' as a closed holiday instead of 'Sunday'. Girls came to school covering their heads with headscarves.

As I had studied earlier in a town-school and prepared for the competitive entrance exams my knowledge base was much wider than the students studying in my class in this new school. I soon came face to face with different boys' gangs in the school and soon found myself along with my friends defending ourselves from the onslaught of these gangs. My studies were suffering and my father was not too happy with my staying at home in such a crucial time of my life when my Matriculation examination was less than two years away. I left home once again for Rajgir.

I was admitted in *R.D.H.*[16] High School, Rajgir. It was beginning of a new life for me. This time I lived in a school hostel but almost independently. I had found the freedom to do things that I had not done in the early school days. I loved watching movies and so far I had been denied to watch as many as I wanted. I just took on them head-on. I bunked classes

---

[15] A great poet who later actively propagated the idea of 'Pakistan' as a home for the Moslems of India

[16] Ramrikh Dass Himmatsingh

every alternate day and watched movies in a
video-hall[17]. It was the only way to watch
movies in the town those days as there was
not a single cinema hall in this small town yet.
I sometimes watched two movies a day
consecutively one after the other.

A year thus passed by and I found myself
at pits in my studies. I was very nervous about
writing the ninth standard exam. I had no clue
how would I pass it. I managed to pass it
somehow but the result of the exam alerted
my father. He became concerned about my
future and advised me to put all my energies
to pass matriculation with a distinction if I
wanted to have a good future at all. It was
almost impossible for me in such a short time
to get a distinction but at times I thought I
could do it for my father's sake whom I loved
and respected so much and who loved me even
more. My father advised me to take private
tuitions from the same teachers who taught at
the R.D.H High School for all the ten subjects
that were part of the Secondary School Board
syllabus viz.-Physics, Chemistry, Biology,
Geography, History, Civics, Hindi, English,

---

[17]   A video-hall is a place where a movie is played on
    television screen by Video Cassette Player

Sanskrit and Mathematics. This was the only way to catch up with my classmates in the school and make up for the lost time.

It was a difficult time and it became even more difficult when I was informed that my Grandma had passed away. I return home with a heavy heart to see her for the last time. I could not bear seeing her so calm and silent. Whenever I visited my ancestral home she hugged me, plucked fresh guavas and mangoes from the orchard, took me around the sugarcane fields and told me stories at night. I touched her soft hands, her long fingers, the fingers I used to hold while walking when I was a little kid. After all our close relatives had paid their last respects to my Grandma, her body was taken to the banks of the sacred Ganges and cremated. I sobbed and sobbed. I had lost someone I very dearly loved.

It took me some time to get over the death of my Grandma and once I was back to normal emotional state I started taking tuitions for Mathematics, Physics, Biology, Chemistry, Sanskrit and English. My father's Hercules bicycle that he had got as gift from his father in law came handy to me. I could go from tuition to tuition quickly on my bicycle. I made a very demanding routine for myself studying sixteen hours a day, sleeping as less as five hours a day and exercising regularly for half an hour to keep myself fit and motivated. I also started going to a nearby temple every evening as going there strengthened my hopes and convictions that a distinction was not impossible.

Our Sanskrit teacher was very experienced and had great teaching skills. Over the years he had mastered the ways to teach Sanskrit and I found his teaching very systematic and easy. It was easy to learn such a difficult subject with him. I soon started performing well in the tuition classes and was learning faster and better than other students. This brought to me a lot of confidence in myself and I started transferring this new found confidence in learning and mastering other subjects. English scared me. I had not learned much English in the primary and middle school except translating simple sentences. I really felt shaky when it came to learning English. Then somehow I managed to locate the English teacher who used to teach me earlier in Gyan Niketan. He agreed to tutor me but his tuition fee was much higher than the other teachers.

We began from the basics. I developed a very good rapport with him and he liked teaching and spending his time with me. In the evening we went to the *kund* for a hot water bath riding his bicycle. During that time we tried to converse in English as much as we could and revised whatever I learned earlier in the day. I had found a friend in him and this really helped as in month's time I had started feeling comfortable in reading English text books.

Mathematics was a difficult subject too. It needed daily practice and I could not do it alone. I needed someone to practice it with me and it was a very dear friend *Ajit*, who came forward to help me. He was good at mathematics and I requested him to practice with me. He gladly agreed and I amazingly improved myself in solving theorems, algebra, and trigonometry. I must say even a math-teacher would not have been as helpful as Ajit proved to be in improving my confidence that I could score well in mathematics. I don't really know where he is these days but he must be a practicing doctor somewhere as he always wanted to be a doctor.

I took tuitions for science subjects too and improved slowly with long hours of self study.

History, Geography and Civics were the most difficult subjects for me. I had to remember dates, places, kings, wars, treaties, climate, crops, biomes etc. My lack of interest in these areas showed up in my final results when I scored the lowest in these subjects. Those days I had tremendous interest in science and science fiction. Biology really excited me and genetics was my favourite. I wanted to know more about DNA, genes, how babies were born, about the possibilities of life in the outer space, how life started on the earth, the prospects of cloning, putting life on other planets and much more. It was genuine joy to learn that the man is responsible for the sex of the child and not the woman as everyone believed in my village that it was the woman who was responsible for the sex of the child. When a man had only baby girls one after the other he remarried to have a baby boy. I thought their ideas to be ridiculous after learning that only the man has the Y chromosomes, the chromosome responsible for the sex of the child. Finding this truth excited me a great deal and I decided to study biology and enlighten the simple villagers with my knowledge about the wonders of science. Later I took Biology as the main subject in Intermediate and I studied mathematics as an additional subject.

I worked very hard for a year for my father's sake as he loved me a lot and wanted me to do well in the Matriculation exam. It was the very first grand task my father and the time had put before me and I had to prove my self to move ahead in my life. It was a 'do or die' situation. I realized that **'it needs discipline, determination and perseverance to achieve even simple things in life.'**

Those days I regularly went to the temple in the evening for meditation and prayers. It really helped me to stay focused and hopeful. I used to transfer the responsibilities of doing well in exam to God while I concentrated on my work.

The dates of the exam were finally announced. It was a ten days 'marathon'. Everyday two papers had to be written. Around ten of us had formed a group to commute to Biharshariff, the district headquarter of Nalanda to write the matriculation exam. We hired a *trekker*[18] together for the next ten days to take

---

[18]   A four wheeler medium sized vehicle that runs well on rough roads

us to the exam centre and back. We stood with each other in those trying times. The exam began at ten in the morning and after three hours we had a lunch break. During the lunch-hour we gathered together, ate lunch together and tried to motivate each other for a better performance during the second session. 'I have good memories of those ten days full of courage, friendship, team spirit, excitement, thrill and joy. I did my best leaving the rest to examiners and God.'

After the exams got over we anxiously waited for the results. I was not sure what was going to come out of it though I was satisfied with the way I had written the exam. I came back home to live with my parents. At home I walked on the top of the roof of my house thinking about the future, looking at the stars in the moonlit nights, wondering if I could ever shine like them. I often dreamed to study science in a prestigious college in the state capital *Patna*[19]. During this time I even thought about the problems of education in my village as many of my school mates in the

---

[19] An ancient city on the banks of the Ganges earlier called Patliputra

primary and middle schools had dropped out. They could not afford private tuitions and thus could not pass matriculation exam.

After a few months results were declared and it surprised us all. I turned out to be the third topmost scorer in the whole High School. No one had ever imagined that including myself. It was my gift to my father who always wanted me to pass matriculation with a distinction. Two girls were ahead of me in the top scorers' list. They were daughters of my teachers who taught at the R.D.H. high-school.

Life felt like a real high and I looked at future with great expectations. After such unbelievably good results I wanted to study in a prestigious college in the state capital Patna but my father thought otherwise. He thought it would be better if I stay with my brother at the district headquarter in Biharshariff and study in *Nalanda College*[20], a college named after the ancient *University of Nalanda*[21]. I rejected the idea at the very outset as I already had the experience of staying there with my brother

---

[20] The best college in Biharshariff
[21] Seat of ancient Nalanda University built around 5A.D. ruins of the university is a major tourist destination

earlier. The idea of staying in a small town greatly constrained my imagination.

Somehow I convinced my father to accompany me to Patna to find me a hostel or one room accommodation where I could live and continue my studies. We went to Patna looking for a suitable accommodation but we could not find any place at the end of the day and we had to return home by the late night bus.

I was very disappointed about not finding a place to stay in the State capital. My father understood this well so the next week we went to Patna again. This time we found a room shared by another two students. Once we found a place to live we started looking for a coaching institute that helped students to prepare for the competitive entrance exams to enter the medical colleges of India. Soon we found a *coaching institute*[22] nearby the dormitory that coached students for the medical entrance examination.

Once I got settled in Patna I applied for admission in two of the best colleges for their

---

[22]   An institute that helps students to prepare for competitive entrance exam viz. medical, engineering, civil services etc.

science courses, Patna Science College and B.N. College and started preparing for the All India Medical Entrance Examination. Despite standing third in the high school and securing seventy eight percent in the matriculation exam I could not secure an admission in any of the two prestigious colleges of the Patna University. I did not want to study in any other college. So I decided to study the Intermediate syllabus on my own along with preparing for the medical entrance exam with the help of the coaching institute.

Patna was a new place and I found it interesting. I often went to the banks of the river Ganges in the evenings and just sat there for hours looking at the ever flowing sacred waters of this ancient holy river and listening to the chirping of the birds. The ambience on the left bank of the Ganges in the evening could best be described as spiritual and sublime in which one could lose oneself in the infinite universe. One cannot forget those moments of peace, solitude, union with the infinite. While returning from the river bank I saw young boys and girls enjoying skating on the grounds of the very old Patna College. Skating excited me and I too learned how to skate it in a short time. Later I spent my evenings in Patna either skating or sitting on the banks of the river Ganges.

Thus a year had passed by and I had not learned much. Most of my time went into watching movies, skating, roaming the bazaars and streets of this ancient city and on the banks of the river Ganges. I had not got myself admitted in any other college as I wanted only the best or nothing. At the end of the year I had not taken admission in Intermediate course in any college and thus had wasted one complete academic year. This worried my father a great deal. The next year I tried again to secure admission in one of the two most prestigious colleges of the Patna University. I had already wasted a year. Now it was 'now or never' situation. Luckily I was admitted in the *B.N. College*[23] for Intermediate course in science. My life once again was back on track but a crucial academic year had been lost.

At the college I made new friends but most importantly I met Shri R.N. Shukla, a

---

[23]   Bihar National College founded in the early twentieth century

Chemistry Reader[24] who was not only a Reader but turned out to be a friend, philosopher and guide. He always tried to motivate us with his encouraging words. Once I visited his home and saw how successfully he ran a school for the children. His friendliness inspired me and later I shifted to his house as a paying guest. He always tried to motivate and encourage me and I worked hard simultaneously preparing for the medical entrance exam as well as the Intermediate exam.

Everyday I attended classes, worked in the laboratories and enjoyed walking along the banks of the river Ganges during the breaks. Time passed by swiftly and the dates of the medical entrance exam for different medical colleges were announced. This time I had to travel to different cities in India to appear at medical entrance exams. I travelled to *Lucknow*[25] and New Delhi all alone. I was not very satisfied with my performance in these exams. Nevertheless I was very happy travelling to distant cities on my own.

---

[24] An academic designation between a lecturer and a professor
[25] The capital city of India's most populous state Uttar Pradesh

After a few weeks the results were declared and turned out to be disappointing as my hunch was. I could not make it to any of the medical colleges, inside or outside Bihar. But my Intermediate exam result was exciting. The best part about it was that it had been declared in due time for the first time in many years. Usually the results were delayed by several months and students lost a year if they wanted to take admission anywhere outside the state particularly in the universities located in the national capital New Delhi. Timely results thus enabled me to apply for admissions in the different colleges of Delhi University in the same session without the loss of a year.

I had heard a great deal about Delhi University and its famous colleges from an acquaintance of my elder brother. He had returned to Patna from New Delhi to prepare for Civil Services examination after graduating in Mathematics from *Hansraj College,* one of the well known colleges of the Delhi University. Besides that I often read in the English national dailies about the amazing campus life in the north campus of Delhi University. Failure in the medical entrance exams had certainly disappointed me but it had cleared the way for me to go to the Delhi University and opened the doors for a promising career in the Indian Civil Services.

A career in the India Civil Services is considered even today to be very prestigious in India. Graduating from a college of Delhi University seemed to me a sure shot way to enter the Indian Civil Service and at this moment for the first time I thought of preparing for Civil Services exam while studying for a bachelor's degree from Delhi University. I met a few Civil Services aspirants in Patna who had been preparing since the last few years, seeking their guidance to decide the optional subjects for writing the Civil Services exam. I learned from them that the students of the arts and humanities background did better in Civil Services than the students of the science background. I also found that students who write the Civil Services exam with Geography as their optional subject score better than the other subjects. Geography brought relatively higher marks than other subject and I decided to choose Geography over Biology as the optional subject for the Civil Services leaving Biology for the good.

How ironical? I had to leave 'Biology' the subject that I loved so much in the High School & Intermediate for 'Geography' the subject that did not interest me at all in the High School. I had made this choice for a better future. "I believe 'life is an irony itself'. We make the most logical and rational choices and decisions that at a later date sound incomprehensible to ourselves and at times when we look back we find them so outrageous and funny in the hindsight."

My elder brother had his own journey from the Paimar to the Ganges. We studied together in the same school started by our father in the beginning and we played in the same fields. My father wanted to give my brother good education and he got him admitted in a private school in Biharshariff but it was my mother who would not agree to part with him. Mother cried and cried till she got my brother back from the school hostel.

Teachers thought him to be bright kid. My father decided to send me again to the school where he had studied earlier. He stayed at home with mother as she wanted and then he was sent to the *Laranpur*[26] High School where my father had earlier studied. The only difference this time was that he was going to live in the high school hostel instead of commuting miles on feet everyday.

My elder brother helped my father plough and irrigate the fields. He was very skilled at repairing things and he could repair radios, water pumps etc. with ease. With his help father was able to produce a lot more rice and wheat than earlier. The two pairs of oxen were sold and my father soon took a loan from the bank to buy a tractor. My elder brother learned quickly how to drive the tractor. Now land could be ploughed with ease and our family earned extra income by renting the tractor to other farmers to plough their land. Later my father hired a driver for operating the tractor. This made my brother free from the house chores. He started concentrating on his studies once again.

Two years later he passed matriculation examination with first division. This was the first time anyone in my village had passed

---

[26] A large village located on the banks of the river Paimar about five kilometers away from Bhattubigha

Matriculation exam with a first division and my elder brother had done that despite putting his energies in helping father in the fields. My father was delighted because his eldest son had not only done better than him but done it despite all barriers, all difficulties. He advised him to take admission in the Nalanda College in the district headquarters at Biharshariff and prepare for the competitive engineering entrance examinations for entering the best engineering colleges for India.

My brother took admission in Biharshariff and at the same time he went to Patna and got admitted in a coaching institute that coached students for the engineering entrance examination. After passing Intermediate in science my brother permanently moved to Patna and devoted his all time and energy to preparing for the various engineering entrance examination.

He gave his best and took a number of attempts at various engineering entrance exams but success eluded him each time. Father advised him to get admitted in a graduate course in any college and simultaneously prepare for the engineering entrance exam.

My brother's Intermediate results were encouraging, he had again passed with a first division, and he took admission in Bachelor degree course in Science for Chemistry in *Kisan College*, Biharshariff. Even after a few more attempts he could not taste any fruits of success so he decided to return to Biharshariff from Patna and to focus on his graduation course.

In Biharshariff he came into the company of his classmates at the Kisan College who had been preparing for a career in banks as bank clerks. The basic degree needed to apply for the clerical job was Intermediate. My brother had an Intermediate degree and he made up his mind to get a job as soon as possible. He joined the banking coaching classes and started travelling to different parts of the country to take these clerical exams. He was always satisfied with his performance in those exams. He also got interview calls many a times after clearing the written main examination, but he could never get past the interview. He was so motivated to get a job in the bank that he ignored his Chemistry classes and as a result he could not pass his annual college examination in Chemistry. He wasted a few vital years of his life in his obsession to become a bank clerk.

3

New Delhi & Delhi University

Give me a firm point on which to stand
And I will move the earth

- Archimedes

I came to Delhi for the first time in 1994 just after passing the matriculation exam. I did not come to Delhi to see *Lal Qila*[1], *Qutub-Minar*[2]

---

[1] Red Fort , built by Mogul emperor Shahjehan
[2] The tallest brick minaret in the world built by Qutb-ud-in Ayibak and his successor Iltutmish in the beginning of the second millennium

Jantar Mantar[3], *Mogul Gardens, 'Rashtrapati Bhawan*[4]*' or the 'Sansad Bhavan*[5]*'* as for what generally people come to Delhi from different parts of the country as well from different countries. I came to Delhi to seek admission in the reputed *Delhi Public School*[6]. Sadly I found the gates of this school closed for a student like me because I had so far studied in the Hindi medium and had obtained less than 90% marks in Matriculation exam conducted by the State Board of Secondary School Examinations in place of the Central Board of Secondary School Examinations.

Well, I returned from the gates, the guard did not let me in knowing my background. So like every other visitor to this city I also went for sight seeing and returned to Patna. I thought my Delhi-Dream had ended and I would never come back to this city again. But the story did not end there. I applied for admission in various colleges of Delhi University after my

---

[3]   A monument built to study astronomy by Maharaja Jai Singh II of Jaipur in 1724
[4]   Presidential Palace
[5]   National Parliament
[6]   A chain of schools run privately all over India in cities but called public schools

Intermediate exam results had been declared. My father was concerned about my going to Delhi and expressed his anxieties. He said... "Delhi is too far son and I won't be able to come there to see you." I said..."Papa, Delhi is so near, just an overnight journey by train from here, what if I have to go to America one day." He did not answer my question and just expressed unsatisfied silence. When he came to see me off at the station, his eyes kept on looking at me without a blink longer and longer as if he had been capturing my image, the whole of me, to keep me safe in his eyes for ever, as if I was going away on a very long journey... I can still see my father looking at me that way... no one has ever looked at me like that...those eyes still say something to me.

After a night's journey by train from Patna I reached the New Delhi Railway Station all alone. I was given addresses of a few students in Delhi who had been preparing for the Civil Services examination since many years. So far they had no luck. I also had the address of a Priest who earlier taught the children of the Chemistry Reader at Patna and at whose house I lived as a paying guest. First of all I went to the Civil Services aspirants and sought their help in applying for admission to the colleges of the Delhi University. They explained me the way to the University and I set on my path on my own after hiring an *auto-rickshaw*[7]. It was the month of July and the city looked fresh green after the monsoon rains. After half an hour of drive we reached the North Campus of the Delhi University. First of all the *auto-wala*[8] took me to the *Kirori Mal (KM) College*[9]. I had a glance of it from outside as it was closed because of that day being Saturday. I had a look at the other colleges of the North Campus and returned to the students' flat. On Monday I again went to the North Campus and applied for admission in four colleges of the Delhi University. First I applied for Geography in KM College then for Zoology in *Hansraj, Ramjas* and *Hindu*[10] college. I did that to stay on the safer side thinking that if I could not secure admission in the KM College I could

---

[7]   A very popular three wheeler to travel on the roads of Delhi

[8]   Driver of three wheelers that run on the roads of Delhi

[9]   A College in the north campus of Delhi University, famous for its celebrity alumni Amitabh Bachchan

[10]   Other reputed colleges of the north campus Delhi University

still keep preparing for the medical entrance exam.

After applying into these colleges I went to meet the priest. He had all the characteristics of a perfect host. He cooked delicious food but had no family. He lived in a single room apartment in the southern part of the city. He had good knowledge of Sanskrit and made his living reciting mantras and conducting *Pujas*[11] in the homes of the rich of the city.

I struck a chord with him in the beginning itself. It seemed to me that he had since long been waiting for a company and I just filled in that gap. In the morning we went for a walk in the nearby park where he collected fresh leaves from the *apple wood tree*[12] for using them in rituals during the '*Pujas*'. During the day he went out for conducting the prayers while I read books. In the evening we went to a nearby temple for the prayers. After the prayers we ate *zalebis*[13] in a roadside restaurant while

---

[11] Worships' rituals, ceremonies
[12] The leaves of the apple wood trees are considered sacred and used in daily prayers and worship of lord Shiva
[13] Circular tasty sweets made from fermented flour all over India and wherever Indians live

returning home. We talked about the life in our common home state 'Bihar', its roads and compared it with life and roads in Delhi.

The Priest showed me many places in the city and I visited many book shops along with him. Earlier while I was still in Intermediate I had heard a lot about Stephan Hawkins and his famous book *'A brief history of time'*. I could not buy it then in Patna. I had plenty of time while waiting for the publication of the admission list of the colleges of the Delhi University so I bought a copy of 'A brief history of time' and got lost into the mysteries of space and time.

The Priest was a remarkable person. He was a complete stranger to me but he turned out to be the best person in the moment of need. "In life sometimes strangers prove to be more helpful than the known relatives or friends." He helped me in the most crucial period of my life and I would always be indebted to him for his kindness. I don't know where the world would head without the kindness and compassion of such million souls who are unknown, insignificant but yet prove vital in adding meaning and comfort to our lives from time to time.

I found love
In the strange people I met
In the strange places,
I gave love
And received love
There was always a helping hand
That came up to hold me
Every time I needed it
And helped keep me going,
I met all kind of people
Good, bad, jealous, virtuous
In the journey of life
Some one or the other
Guided me through the path,
How may I pay back?
For their love and kindness
How may I give back more
Than I ever took

I had stayed at his place for more than fifteen days waiting for the cut off list for admission in Delhi University. Time just flied in the learned company of the Priest. The first cut off list for admission had already been published in the newspapers. I eagerly looked at the first cut off list in the newspaper. Sadly, my percentage of marks did not fall within it as the cut off was eighty-five percent and higher for getting admitted in *B.A. (H)*[14] in Geography in the KM College.

The admissions in the colleges of Delhi University were based on the cut-off percentage marks system. That meant that the students who had obtained certain percentage marks above a cut off percentage in their secondary school exams were to be offered admissions first. If all the seats were not filled in the first cut-off then they would publish a second cut-off percentage marks lower than the first cut off percentage marks. Generally by the third cut-off percentage marks all seats got filled.

After a week the second cut off list of Delhi University was published. The second cut-off list for Zoology of the *Ramjas College*[15] offered me admissions but my heart lied in Geography at the KM College. I decided to wait for another

---

[14]   Bachelor of Arts with Honors
[15]   A college located in   the North Campus, Delhi University

week for the third cut-off list. Happily my percentage marks were within the third cut-off list for B.A (H) in Geography at the KM College. My eyes could not believe it. I rushed to the college admission counter with all the necessary documents. The section-officer who was checking and verifying the papers looked at me and said ... "These are fake certificates". My heart sank. I could not think for a while but then I gathered all my energy and asked – "why do you say so"? He replied –"Because these certificates are from Bihar". He was direct and blunt in his reply. This was a clear case of stereotyping and discrimination on the regional basis. I challenged him if he could prove that my certificates were falsified or fake. He advised me to get it verified from proper authorities who sat in the corner room at the ground floor of the KM College. I ran here and there looking for the corner room and the 'proper authorities' and in the end somehow managed to locate them. I showed them my certificates for verification. They looked at them carefully and said- "they are all right" and put the stamp of verification on them. I felt relieved. I walked back to the section-officer and resubmitted the verified certificates. He had no choice but to admit me in the College now.

After I was admitted I was so happy that words would not do justice here. It was a new life for me perhaps one of the best gifts I had ever got in my life. I went back to the Priest, thanked him for his help and kindness and for being such a great company and host. Classes were due to start in the middle of August next month so I packed up my bags and left for home to see my parents. I told my parents about my admission in a prestigious college of the Delhi University and they were delighted to hear this news. Papa offered me to give all the money I needed to complete my graduation. After a general discussion Papa agreed to send me a sum of Rs. 3000 (around US $70) every month besides the additional expenses for admission fees and purchasing books from time to time. After a good holiday I returned to New Delhi in the first week of August 1997 with a lot of dreams to start a new life in a new city. The Priest again helped me to find a one room apartment near the KM College. He also found me a caterer who brought me my meals everyday.

Delhi has some kind of invisible energy in its ambience. Its touch is magical. It transforms you. My first day at the college brought me into an altogether new world. I saw such a beautiful and innocent face that day that I could not forget it for long. That face had hypnotic effects on me. Her name was *Ritika*. For her too it was the first day at the college. We were going to be in the same class for the next three years but three years felt so short from the very first day. I eagerly looked forward to see her in the class everyday. I became one of the most regular students in the college. In some time I learned that she was not only beautiful but had a brilliant mind too. She had scored around ninety percent in her senior secondary school examination and could have chosen any given subject at any college of the Delhi University. What impressed me most was that she had chosen to study Geography despite being the daughter of a History professor and a very well known Historian of India. Her father taught at the Delhi University and had written a few books on ancient Indian history. She soon joined *'The Players'*[16] and started

_____

[16] The drama society of the KM College, Delhi University

acting in plays based on various themes. She acted brilliantly and even earned awards for her performance in plays. She was an inspiring person who lived her life with an attitude... "Take life as it comes" while I believed in ... "Better plan it". Though I had completely different attitude for living my life I truly valued and respected her attitude. I never compared the two.

I did not have much liking for Geography in the school days. This was the subject I had scored the lowest in the matriculation exam. I had not even read a word of Geography in the last three years so I was not sure about my performance in the exam. Most of the other students in my class had studied Geography in the senior secondary school while I had to start from the scratch. This was a challenging task for me. Nevertheless I had a very straight and clear goal in my head to secure a career in the Indian Civil Service by competing in the Civil Services exam. Another major immediate challenge for me was to improve my written and spoken English. I had studied in Hindi medium till matriculation and had shifted to English medium only in the Intermediate. Limited knowledge of English was sufficient for the Intermediate. Now it was a completely different setting in the North Campus of Delhi University. Most of my new classmates communicated well in English as they had their schooling in the English medium. I and *Bajrang*[17] Singh Rathode from Nagore district of the state of *Rajasthan*[18] were the only two exceptions. We became good friends and studied together for the next three years until Bajrang left for *Jaipur*[19] and I continued in Delhi.

Language plays a very important role in our lives and particularly English language in India where only a minority of people can understand and speak it. Due to our colonial past, just to communicate in English is a social statement in itself. The knowledge of English can help one to get the creamy jobs and has huge economic advantages. This is reflected in the teaching of this language in the different schools and the education system itself.

---

[17] Bajrang is name of one of monkey Gods in the Hindu mythology
[18] A state in western India, land of Rajas and Maharajas
[19] Capital of the state of Rajsthan also known as the Pink City

India's education system even today remains clearly divided. One the one side are the government schools where the medium of teaching is either Hindi or the other vernacular languages with very little emphasis on English while on the other side are the Convent schools run by the Christian missionaries or the Private schools, often called Public schools, a misnomer, run by the private bodies where the medium of instruction is generally English. This divide becomes even starker because of the socio-economic profile of the two types of schools. The first set of schools caters to the rural masses and the urban poor while the other set caters to the well-offs in the society, mostly the urban middle class. The two schools produce very different kind of students with very different outlooks and preferences. The gap between the two gets wider with time.

I came face to face with this great divide for the first time when I was admitted in the KM College, Delhi University. The medium of instruction here was English and most of my classmates came from the second set of schools. It created a difficult situation for me. I just felt that 'I don't belong here'. It was perhaps the first cultural shock of my life. For a while I felt

like running far away from the classroom,
somewhere I could feel and be comfortable,
somewhere I belonged to. Fortunately there
was no turning back and I stayed on. Perhaps
I was adapting fast. I started to work on my
English by regularly reading the English
national dailies. In Delhi almost all aspirants
for a career in the Civil Services read one or
the other English dailies like The Hindu, The
Times of India or The Hindustan Times. I started
with The Hindu, a relatively serious newspaper
for an average reader but essential for the *Civil
Services aspirants*[20]. Reading it was pure
education for me. I continuously needed to look
for the meaning of the new words in a
dictionary. I bought a copy of the 'Twenty-first
Century Chamber's Dictionary' to assist me in
reading the English newspaper. In a few
months my English language vocabulary had
improved significantly. The next step was to
try conversing in English with whomever I
could, as much as I could. I tried it with the
other students in my class and in the college.
They must be getting bored with my adventures
in a foreign tongue but I had no choice but to

---

[20] Students who aspire to have a career in the prestigious
      Indian Civil Services

venture out, take risks, and suffer embarrassments.

I had also started working on my Geography along with my English. I thoroughly studied the *NCERT* [21] Geography books from the standard sixth to twelfth. It helped me a great deal to boost up my confidence to face the first annual college examination in Geography. Lecturers in the College were very supportive. *Mrs. Seema Parihar* was one of them. She taught Cartography to the first year students in the Geography department of the KM College. She did not only teach us the subject matter but also encouraged us to participate in the extra-curricular activities in and out of the college. I still remember well what she told us one day in a class room gathering. She said- **"Widen your horizons"**. These were just three words but had magical effect on me. These magical words have always inspired me since then to do better, to try something new and to soar higher and higher in life.

I slowly got accustomed to the campus life in the Delhi University. I did not feel running

---

[21]   National Council of Education, Training and Research

away anymore. Slowly I started feeling that at ease with this amazing world. Soon I discovered the beautiful *'Rose Garden'*[22] dedicated to Pundit Jawaharlal Nehru, India's first Prime Minister, in front of the office of the Vice Chancellor of the Delhi University. All colours of roses bloomed here in the 'Rose Garden, giving this place of learning a beautiful look and rosy smell. The *Buddha Jayanti Park*[23] was located nearby the 'Rose Garden' where young lovers spent their evenings in the shadows of the large trees. Just opposite of my College stood the red sand stone building of the reputed *Delhi School of Economics*[24] where once the Nobel laureate in Economics Professor Amartya Sen taught. It was just D-school for us. We often frequented its canteen during the lunch break where the whole world of geographical and political thought was discussed over a cup of *chai*[25] and a plate of *sambhar-vada*[26] with Dr. Majumdar, our

---

[22] A garden of roses located in North Campus, Delhi University

[23] A park located at the North Campus ,Delhi University

[24] Delhi School of Economics is one of the centers of excellence in the field of economics

[25] Ttea

[26] A delicious South Indian dish

evergreen Scholar College Reader. A morning
jog in the University stadium refreshed and
energized me for the whole day. An evening
stroll in the lush green Buddha Jayanti Park
with fresh smells of herbs filled up my senses.
The breathtaking sights of the chirping birds
flying home while the red sun set in the western
skies filled me with transcendental joys. In those
evenings of solitude I thought of India and her
place in the world and how diplomacy could
help to make a better world. During those
moments a sense of calm prevailed upon me
and my soul sang in ecstasy-

I was always there

As the blowing wind

Or the falling leaves,

As the shining sun

Or the flowing streams,

As the chirping birds

Or the blooming buds,

As the blue sky

Or the empty space

I was never born

I did not die...

The beautiful face I had seen on the first day at College had stayed in mind. She was always there in my thoughts. We saw each other everyday but did not say much except 'hello'. One day we met in the library and I told her... "I have to ask you something."

She said- "go ahead, please ask".

I thought better to put it on paper so I said- "I'll write down it for you."

She smiled and said- "please do it".

I quickly wrote on the paper. I folded the paper and handed it over to her. I told her to think about it and then I left. The next time we met she did not even smile. I asked her about the paper I had given to her. She said-"what kind of question is that 'why do we exist and why are we here on the earth'?" I never think about such things and don't want to even think about it. Have you got no other work or what, except thinking such deep philosophical absurdities? Her answer completely flattened me. I did not dare to talk to her for many days. I rather focused on improving my English and Geography.

By the end of the year I felt comfortable in Geography and was ready to write the annual college examination. Before the annual exam every year the College's foundation day was celebrated. On this day the awards were given to the students who had performed well in the preceding academic year in various faculties' viz. academics, sports, debates, drama, music, social work, NCC[27] etc. On this day I saw many students, who had performed with excellence last year in any given area, walking up to the stage for receiving the award amidst the renting clap of a large number of students, shaking hand with the Principal of the College and the with the Chief guest. Afterwards they said a few words underlining that they would continue to perform with excellence in the future as well. For a moment I imagined my self there on the stage. It felt nice but I could imagine the hard work it needed to be there.

Soon it was exam time and students were seen heading towards the library frantically. Soon once empty library was crowded for the first time in the year. I revised whatever I had studied throughout the year. She had consistently performed better than me in class while participating in other extra curricular

---

[27] National Cadet Corps

activities at the same time. I thought I could at least beat her in the annual college examination.

She prepared with her friends while I did it on my own. Exams started and got over. Papers were easy and I did not have much problem in writing the exam in English medium. In fact it was an easy sail. When the last paper of our annual college examination got over she invited me for the first time to her home along with her other friends for lunch.

I saw the room she lived in. It was very well done up. In the corner of the room a bookshelf stood full of books of all kinds. Perhaps she had put all the books she had collected since her childhood in that shelf. On the table lied a music-system that played songs of Bob Dylan and John Denver. I wanted to meet her parents. I had heard a lot about her father and it was an opportunity for me to talk to him. Her mother was a very sweet lady and a perfect host. She prepared a delicious lunch for us and served us herself. Her father, the History Professor looked a bit serious person as perhaps a History Professor should be and a after a small talk on the luncheon table we got along quiet well with each other. After a good lunch we decided to go for a movie at *Shakuntalam theatre*[28] . We watched "You have got mail" starring Tom Hanks and Meg Ryan that day. This was the first Hollywood movie I had ever seen in my life. I was only able to make sense of just half the words spoken in American accent but it was fun to go out with her and her friends. Thus my first year at the college had passed. It had passed by so fast that it seemed to me as if I had entered the College just yesterday.

The College had got closed for the summer vacation. Most of the students had left for their homes. I too wanted to go home but instead I decided to use this time to improve my English speaking skills by joining the *British Council*[29] in New Delhi. The course duration was just 32 hours spread over 16 days and it cost me a huge sum of Rs. 4200 (~US $100). I asked Papa's opinion and he gave me a go-ahead signal by sending me the required money by

---

[28]   A movie hall named after the great literary work of the Great Kalidas, 'Abhigyan Shakuntalam' located in Pragati Maidan , India's largest exhibition center

[29]   The cultural wing of the British diplomacy that promotes the English language through teaching courses and libraries

the post in form of a bank draft. The post got delayed in reaching me and I had to borrow money from someone to get admission in the British Council in due time.

Over the course of time I had come to know Rajesh *Bhaiya*[30] who had been preparing for Civil Services examination in Delhi since the past few years with Geography as one of his optional papers. He regularly guided me how to prepare for the civil services examination. He was the only person I could ask for the needed money for the admission. I turned to him and asked him to lend me the required sum for a very short period of time till my post arrived. He lent me the required money for a short duration to get admission in the language course offered by the British Council.

The course attracted persons from all age groups. I stood somewhere in the middle. We played language games, tried to converse with each other and focus on the correct pronunciation of the English words. The course was just for the sixteen days and soon it ended. Though the 16 days-32 hours-US100$ course

---

[30] Elder brother, a term used while addressing someone with respect

did not do anything substantial to help me in improving my communication skills in English, it did provide me the confidence to use the language without hesitation. This was all I needed, I guess, to move on.

After the course got over I visited my parents and my grandpa. It was almost towards the end of the summer vacation at the Delhi University and I could only spend a very few days with my parents as the summer vacation. My father was very happy to know that I had made good use of the vacation time and successfully completed the English language course at the British Council. He always emphasized on the point of 'making good use of the vacation time as one can only get ahead of the others while they rest and one leaps forward.' My father eagerly looked forward to my annual college examination results. I visited my Grandpa just for a day and returned to New Delhi as I had very little time left before the classes again started in the College. The results had already been declared when I returned to New Delhi. I had scored a magnificent seventy percent and was the fifth top scorer in the class; three girls and a boy were ahead of me including Ritika. I was very happy for myself but happier for her. I always thought she deserved it.

The outcome of the good results was that now I could get to stay in the college hostel. It could save my money as I did not have to pay huge rent hiring a flat outside as I had been paying since last eleven months. The KM College hostel mess could provide me my meals. I applied for a seat in the College Hostel and I got it without much hassles.

The second year students had to share a room with another student. I had been allotted a room with a *Bangladeshi*[31] student 'Kamrul Hassan'. Kamrul was a third year student of the English literature and was a book worm. Despite working so hard he never scored well in the annual college exams. He was averse to listening music while he studied and once he dashed my new radio on the floor when I played some music while he was studying. Though he got it repaired afterwards but the broken radio always reminded me of the time I had spent with book worm Kamrul. He was not unkind though. He introduced me to his Bangladeshi friends, especially Haque whose

---

[31]   A person from Bangladesh

bag I borrowed later while going to Manila for the World Universities Debating Championship. Kamrul had also treated me to dinner once and once we had even watched a movie together. He had a crush on an Indian girl or was it the other way round and Kamrul used to open his heart to me from time to time.

Things never get to be perfect in life. While getting hostel solved my problems of food and money it brought me face to face with ragging in my initial few days in the College hostel and later with the naked practice of *casteism*[32] and regionalism among the residents of the hostel. The occurrence of such thing in such a prestigious college of the Delhi University shocked me because I had thought that these were the village issues but ironically I found villages had better social ambience than a Delhi University College hostel.

A few rough guys wanted to rag me so they knocked at the door after the midnight and asked me to come out of my room. Kamrul protested against it but they did not pay heed to it. I had to come out at night woken up

---

[32]   The practice of discrimination on the basis of a person's caste

from my sweet sonorous sleep. They asked me to say some funny things, get naked and fetch water for them from the ground floor to the first floor, do push ups and clean up their dirty rooms and put things in order etc. They were very curious to know what caste did I belong to but did not dare ask me directly. So they kept on going round and round asking my father's name and my grandfather's name etc. so they could at least catch something from their surnames. For them my surname 'Kumar' was of no help as it is a caste neutral surname. I did not think it dignifying to tell them my caste or ask them their caste. They kept on guessing for the next two years but never got a clue.

The hostel residents were divided on the basis of the regional affinities in three groups-*Biharis*[33], *Jats*[34] *and Chinkis*[35]. *Biharis* were once again divided into two groups –the backward caste group and the forward caste group on the basis of caste. During the elections for the College hostel President these deep fissures

---

[33] Students and people from the state of Bihar
[34] People from the state of Haryana
[35] People from the north-eastern states of India

surfaced when various strategic alliances were worked out to win the Presidential election. This kind of petty politics irritated me and I wanted to keep myself far away from all these. I had joined the hostel to study and to devote more time to extra-curricular activities. I did not want to be a part of any narrow minded politics based on caste and regional groups. So I kept out of the petty politics of the College hostel and the College and focused on the studies, debates, social work and other extra curricular activities.

4

XIXth World Universities Debating Championship, Manila, Philippines

It is not weapons that strike down the foe
It is wisdom that in the end lays him low

-Panchatantra

In the beginning of my second year at the college after returning from my home I became a member of the Debating Society (DebSoc) and took active part in Inter-college debating events. DebSoc was led by a very warm person full of wit and humour, Siddhartha Suryanarayan who was a year senior to me in the College. He had been to Rome, the last year to represent the KM College in the World Universities Debating Championship and had been awarded on the College Foundation Day the last year for his excellent performance in debating. He was an able leader and helped us to prepare for the tough debates. Siddhartha had his eyes on the upcoming nineteenth world universities debating championship to be held in Manila, Philippines in the end of 1998. He wanted to prepare and send a good team to the world debates at the end of the year. I had just joined the *DebSoc*[1] and I was ready to work hard. Though I did not think of making it to Manila that year I was giving my best and was improving day by day. During the most part of the first year in the College I had spent my time reading English newspapers to improve my English language skills. It had a very useful side-effect on me as my knowledge of the Indian and World Affairs substantially improved during that period and I developed a very good knowledgebase of facts and figures

---

[1]   Debating Society

in polity and economy. This often helped me a great deal in debates. My English language communication skills were not as great as Siddhartha's or some of the other members of the DebSoc but my strong knowledgebase gave the whole debate the due weight and effect. Siddhartha had noted in the last World Debates that what was really needed during the testing hours was a debater who had a vast knowledgebase as well as good communication skills and not just a phoney chatterbox talking in the air. Finally when the time came to select the KMC Team for the World Universities Debating Championship there were many aspirants and contenders from the DebSoc. Only five out of fifteen were going to make it to Manila. Siddhartha had decided to give himself a break this time and let the new debaters have the opportunity to go to the World Debates, a hallmark of his great leadership qualities. After consulting with the College authorities he prepared a test to measure both written and verbal skills of the debaters. I performed excellently in the written test. It was a gruelling test and I stood third in it. My scores in the communication skills test were not bad. This helped me to get into the team to represent KM College in the nineteenth World Universities Debating Championship in Manila. We practiced together wherever and whenever we could, in the College, at Siddhartha's home, we practiced even on the Sundays. We had managed to convince the Principal to give us the keys of the air-conditioned college seminar room so that we could practice even in the very hot Indian summer months of June and July. Our new Principal Bhim Sen Singh, a former student of the KM College himself was very enthusiastic about the College's participation in a world event and he handed us over the keys of the air conditioned seminar room with pleasure. We practiced everyday for hours and it went on for more than three months.

The World Debating Council (WDC) needed both debaters and the judges to participate in the World Universities Debating Championship. The WDC follows the parliamentary style of debating in which one side is the Government and on the other side is the Opposition. The Government side consists of the Prime Minister, who has the responsibility to introduce the topic and define it, the deputy Prime Minister, a government member and a Whip. The Opposition consists of the Leader of Opposition who speaks against the motion and is assisted by the deputy Leader of Opposition, an opposition member and a Whip. Anyone can stop anybody at any point of time and ask a question starting with "on that point sir". On the judgment panel there is a speaker of the house who presides over the session and is assisted by two judges. In the end of the debating session the Speaker asks for the opinion of the two judges and the marks given by the judges. Finally the average scores of the Speaker and the two judges are submitted to the conducting authorities of the debating championship.

We started the special preparation for the World Debates in September 1998. World Debates were to take place in the December end and we had to work out our travel plans. One day Siddhartha asked us about our travel plans and with a degree of shock and surprise, I think more a degree of shock than surprise, he found that I did not have a passport. He said -'how the hell are you going to go to Manila without a passport?' I had no answer because frankly I did not know that I needed a passport to travel outside India. My parents had never owned a passport and I had never thought that I would travel out of India so soon. I had no clue how to get a passport. I found out that getting a passport could be a lengthy and time taking process and it was very difficult to get a passport at such a short notice. Finally one of my team-mates Amitabh Singh came to my rescue. His parents were *joint-secretaries*[2] in the Central Government of India in New Delhi. I got a letter signed by his father for a *tatkal*[3] passport and applied at the Regional Passport Office at R.K Puram in New Delhi. Within a week's time I received a passport and I was ready to travel.

After getting a passport with one year validity I went to the Philippines Embassy in New Delhi along with other four team mates for the visas. It did not take much time there though an official from the embassy interviewed us before giving us the visas. We bought the air tickets from the Thai Airways for the New Delhi-Bangkok-Manila route transiting through Bangkok, Thailand. The return flight was also

---

[2]   High ranking officials in the Central Government of India

[3]   Immediate issuance of a passport without the police verification with a validity period of just one year

transiting through Bangkok so we decided to visit the Bangkok city on our way back to New Delhi. We went to the Royal Thai Embassy in New Delhi and easily got the visas for Thailand.

The college sponsored almost all the travel and accommodation expenses but we had to contribute Rupees 10,000(~$200) from our own pockets for the personal expenses. I did not have that amount of money with me that time. I asked my father to send me some money but he could not send it immediately. So I had to look for help somewhere else. I turned towards our new College Principal Mr. Bhimsen Singh for help and he was very kind to give me Rs. 5000 with pleasure for a week. I managed to gather the rest Rs. 5000 from my friends and acquaintances.

Now we had to fulfil the specifications of wardrobe laid by the World Debating Council. I needed a formal business suit. I never had one. So I had to get my suit stitched too. Two of my team-mates wanted to get stitched the new ones as well. This time Amitabh's mother came to my rescue. She took us to a *Raymond*[4] Showroom located in the inner circle of the

---

[4]   A popular brand that sells quality clothes for suits

Connaught Place[5] in New Delhi. Raymond had a large variety of suit pieces. We selected the colours; I chose a dark grey colour suit piece and handed it over to the tailor for stitching. We did some shopping from the *Sarojaninagar market*[6] as well. We bought white shirts and formal shoes and many pieces of undergarments as we were going to travel to an island country with hot tropical climatic conditions. We were also supposed to wear our traditional national dress one evening at the debates. I was a bit in a dilemma over choosing my traditional national dress as my father wore *Dhoti-Kurta*[7] but the young people preferred *Sherwani*[8] those days. Finally I bought a *Sherwani* from the *Kamlanagar*[9] market. I did not have enough money left to buy a suitcase so I had no choice but to borrow one and my roommate Kamrul was of great help as he helped me in borrowing a big bag from his friend Haque.

---

[5] Central business district of New Delhi
[6] An open market where one can buy things at cheap rates
[7] A traditional dress worn by men in North India
[8] A popular north Indian traditional dress
[9] A market behind the KM College also known as *Kanax* in the Delhi University lingo

After packing all the necessary items I was ready to leave India for the first time in my life. I was a bit scared of the flight as it was the first flight of my life and I did not want to think about it for the time being. I first went to Amitabh's home in *Chanakyapuri*[10] because his parents wanted to see us off at the airport. We reached the Indira Gandhi International Airport after forty minutes drive from Chanakyapuri. The whole place looked wonderful to me as I was seeing an airport for the first time. I was so happy to see all that but I was a bit sad too as I did not have my parents to see me off at the airport as all the other four of my team-mates had. I was on my own. How much I wished at that moment if my parents could be there waving their hands while I checked in. After checking in and completing the necessary formalities at customs and security points we finally entered the waiting area from where we were to enter the aero plane. We were carrying our suits with us holding in our hands as they could not be put inside the suitcase. After waiting for more than an hour finally we were let inside the plane. The

---

10 An area in New Delhi where top bureaucrats and
    diplomats live

beautiful air hostesses in their colourful floral attires wearing fruity perfumes welcomed us onboard the Thai airways aircraft. The flight safety instructions were read out and the air hostesses demonstrated to us how to wear an oxygen mask in case the air pressure in the cabin dropped down, what to do if plane landed up in sea and how to exit in case of an emergency. This sounded a bit weird to a first time flier like me. It scared me a great deal as thoughts of a plane crash started flashing in my mind. The initial run up and take off was quite scary and I felt pain in my ears because of the air pressure changes. Once the plane was high up in the sky it was smooth.

We had left New Delhi on 27th December night and after two and half hours of flight we reached Bangkok in the very early morning of 28th December. We waited at the Bangkok airport for more than an hour to transit to another plane. It just took an hour and half for us to reach Manila International airport. At the airport a team of volunteers from the Manila University helped us to reach the hotel Shangri-la. A person from the Indian Embassy in Manila had also come to the airport to facilitate our smooth passage at the immigration and customs checkpoints. We were taken to the *hotel Shangri-la*[11] located adjacent to the Asian Development Bank in the centre of the Manila city. The cabs ran smoothly at the speed of 120-140 Km per hour on the way to the hotel from the Manila International Airport. In India I had only heard of such speeds but here I was experiencing the thrill of such speed sitting in the cab that could be called luxurious by the Indian standards. Another interesting thing I noticed on the way to the hotel was that all brands of cars, even very expensive ones were used here as cabs. In India those days all one could get for a taxi was old and rickety *ambassador cars*[12].

Shangri-la was a five star hotel. This was one of the other firsts in my life. My eyes opened to a completely different world there that had perhaps always existed but was completely different from my world, the world I came from, the world I lived in. In the hotel three of us had to share one suite so three of

---

[11] A five star hotel located in the center of the Manila city

[12] A type of car produced by Hindustan Motors mostly used by the government in India and runs as taxis on Indian roads

the younger members of the five member team, Amitabh, Ankur and I shared one big suite. Hotel had put an extra bed in our suite for us. The extra bed was slightly smaller and lower than the bigger double bed. We democratically decided to sleep on the extra bed one by one during the five nights we spent there.

After refreshing ourselves and resting for a while we gathered in the conference room of the hotel. The host Manila University welcomed us all to the Nineteenth World Universities Debating Championship. A test paper was handed over to us to judge our abilities as judges for the debating championship. Three of us made it to the top. Chetan from the mathematics department of our college made it to the top twenty judges for this event. I and Pandey did well too.

In the evening we explored the city a little stepping out of the hotel Shangri-la. We found a Mac Donald outlet in the vicinity. It was the only familiar joint in the area where I could find some vegetarian food to eat. I bought apple pies and French fries for dinner as there was hardly any other choice for the vegetarians and drank coke.

In the morning we all had a heavy breakfast in the hotel as it offered a great range of vegetarian foods and was included in the accommodation bills. Afterwards all the participants in the World Universities Debating Championship were taken to the campus of the Manila University by a bus from the hotel, where the Nineteenth World Universities Debating Championship was formally inaugurated by the Mayor of Manila. Debaters from 127 Colleges, Universities and Institutes from eighty eight countries around the world were participating in this grand event. The first round consisted of preliminaries. In the preliminaries all the participants who had come to debate in the championship were given opportunity to prove their debating skills. The ones who had been selected out of the preliminaries went through the octa-final round of the championship the next day. It was followed up by the quarter-final and semi-final rounds. My team-mates Amitabh and Ankur did reach till the octa-final round but could not make it to the quarter-final round. The competition was really tough as more than half of the participants were the law students from the law faculties of the various reputed

Universities of the world. A number of other Indian Colleges and Institutes were also present in Manila for the debating championship. The St. Stephan College team from the Delhi University, St. Xavier College team from the University of Bombay and IIM A (Indian Institute of Management, Ahmedabad) team could make it to the quarter-finals but they too were thrown out in the semi-finals. I remember Government College Lahore from Pakistan reaching the semi-finals but they too could not make it to the finals. The finals took place in the City Centre in Manila in presence of the erstwhile President of Philippines Mr. Joseph Estrada. The topic for the grand final debate was "This house supports an independent Palestinian State". The final round participants were Cambridge University, UK, Oxford University, UK, John Hopkins University, USA and Monash University, Australia. The debate was won by the Monash University while Cambridge University stood second. We gave a standing ovation to all the four teams as they had performed brilliantly.

After such a great event it was time for the farewell. On this eve a farewell dinner had been organized for all of us by the host Manila

University. For the first time in my life I had
seen and met the students and debaters from
so many countries together. It changed my
thinking and outlook towards my life and
career a great deal. During the five days I
spent in Manila I people from over hundred
nationalities, saw a new city and new life-styles.
I made new friends and promised to keep in
touch with them in the future. One among
them was beautiful Einat from Haifa, Israel.
She studied Psychology at the Haifa University.
We kept in touch for some time but lost it
somehow afterwards nevertheless memories
linger on. A picture still hangs on my wall me
and Einat standing and smiling together saying
farewell to world debates and Manila. John
was another interesting fellow debater from
the University of London, a fellow who just
smiled like me. We got along very well.
Victoria was a law student at the Cambridge
University. I just cannot forget her blue eyes
and talks we had while travelling once in the
bus from the Shangri-la hotel to the Manila
University.

At the last day of our stay in Manila, the
Indian Ambassador to Philippines invited all
the Indian participants at the World Debates

for a dinner. We extended our invitation to the Pakistani debaters to join us for dinner after taking permission of the Ambassador but they did not show up for the dinner.

At eight in the evening we reached the Ambassador's residence. It looked magnificent. We were warmly welcomed by the Ambassador, his wife and the First Secretary. We were soon joined by his two young daughters who studied in France and had come to see their parents during the Christmas vacation. Indian food was served with red wine. I was desperate to eat Indian food as I had been living on fruits, juices, coke, French fries and apple pies since the time I had landed in Manila. Indian food was a great delicacy for me in such circumstances and I had as much as I could. I sat near the Ambassador at the dining table and discussed the India-Philippines and India-ASEAN relations and politics in Philippines. I was just eighteen that time and I wondered what Ambassador might be thinking about my amateur questions and about me. After the dinner my team- mates decided to go to a pub and drink. In their company I too landed up there I tried beer for the first time in my life and soon others found that I was drunk. I managed to get into the car and then I don't remember much. I got up in the morning with a hang-over and it was time to check out of the Shangri la and leave for the airport for Bangkok.

In Bangkok we were received at the airport by an Indian embassy staff and were taken to a hotel in the city centre. The evening we ate dinner at Mac Donald and my team-mates did a little shopping in the big malls. That time those grand shopping venues had just started to appear in Delhi and window shopping in Bangkok in those big malls was a novelty for me. The next day we went for the site-seeing around the city. We found it clean, well-maintained and developed. The economic reforms conducted by the Thai government were showing up in the way the city had come up. We saw many statues of Buddha around the city, visited the Royal Palace where the revered King still lived and a few other sites. We learnt that Thais revere their King. Our one day in Bangkok was over and at night we returned to New Delhi. On the way back the television monitors inside the plane showed the exact cities we were flying over and at one point I found that I was flying over the places very close to my home in Nalanda. I wished I could jump out of the plane with a parachute and just had a glimpse of my parents but wishes are wishes...after an hour I was again at the Indira Gandhi International Airport in New Delhi and no one was waiting for me at the airport to receive me.

These were just seven days of my life but were perhaps equivalent to the seven years of learning. When I look back I feel indebted to KM College for the opportunity it gave to me and to Siddhartha who played the role of a leader so elegantly. Today I have no contacts with him but I am very happy that he has carved a niche for himself. He is, as I have heard, quite a popular actor in South India and has now made a debut in the *Bollywood* as well with a leading role in the much acclaimed film *'Rang De Basanti*[13]*'*. After returning from Manila I decided to work very hard for a career in the Indian Foreign Service which I thought would give me many more such opportunities

---

[13] An Indian film produced in 2006 that calls upon the youth to take inspiration from the young heroes who sacrificed their lives in India's freedom struggle against the British colonial rule in India to deal with today's problems

in the future. Today when I am living my dream I feel how vital the Nineteenth World Universities Debating Championship has been for my life. We were not winners of the Nineteenth World Universities Debating Championship but we had lost nothing in Manila. We had come back enriched and experienced.

5

Beyond the Classroom

Restless, onwards must thou strive
Never halt nor languor know

-Schiller

In the beginning of my second year at the KM College I became a member of National Service Scheme (NSS). NSS was created with an aim to streamline the energies of the Indian youth for the benefit of the society. The NSS team of KM College consisted of three office bearers and a large number of volunteers. As members of NSS we planted trees in the College campus, participated in anti-pollution campaign within the university campus as well as outside the campus. In the week ends we visited 'Nirmal Hirday[1]', a home for the destitute founded by Mother Teresa. We were warmly received by the inmates of 'Nirmal Hirday' who perhaps waited the whole week to interact and play with us.

Once in a year we organized Blood Donation Camp in the College in which the whole College participated with great enthusiasm. The teachers and students turned out in large numbers to donate blood. We made creative posters to spread awareness about HIV, AIDS and practicing safe sex among the College students. NSS volunteers went to the slums to teach the children who could not afford to go to a school. We also organized an annual seminar in which we discussed the issues related to the social and psychological health of the students. We invited a few imminent speakers every year to speak on some burning social issues of the day. Prizes and awards were distributed on this day to the students who had excelled in social work

---

[1]   It translates as 'Clean Heart'. It is run by the Missionaries for Charities founded by Mother Teresa

during the last academic year. I too received the award of excellence before passing out of the College for my services as the Vice President of the NSS, KM College. I always stayed a member of the NSS even when later I moved to the Jawaharlal Nehru University (JNU) for doing post graduation after passing out from the Delhi University. In JNU the NSS was instrumental in making the University campus a litter-free zone. We also strived hard to make the JNU campus a smoke-free zone.

My second year at KM College was full of extra curricular activities. I was very keen to broaden my horizons. During this time three teachers at the College Zini Loknita, Shahana and Somujit Bhattacharya laid the foundation of a Gender Issue Forum to spread awareness among the college students about the forms of gender discrimination prevalent in the University campus and how to address them. I along with Sweta and Momo joined this forum as volunteers as soon as it was founded. The forum was given a popular Hindi name "Parivartan[2]". Parivartan soon hired a professional psychologist for providing

---

[2]   Parivartan means Change

counselling services to the needy students who were victims of gender discrimination. We functioned as a spirited team. Every Wednesday we organized a meeting with the students and teachers of different colleges of Delhi University and encouraged them to share their experiences of gender discrimination in their college campuses. We designed and painted posters to popularize the most common forms of gender discriminations that prevailed in the University campus.

The second year thus turned out to be very hectic for me. I worked more than twelve hours a day to keep up with the demands of DebSoc, NSS and 'Parivartan' besides attending Geography classes. During the first year I had only focused on Geography but in the second year it got the least emphasis and when the exams came close I felt a bit shaky. Though I had attended most of the classes during the whole year I did the final preparation just a week before the exam. I had learned it that in Delhi University one could really score well if one wisely selected a number of most expected questions and just mugged them up in the last few days. I saw ninety percent of the students in my class doing the same and that included some of the top scorers. This year I had no other option except doing exactly what others did. The second year exam came and went away smoothly. The last day of the exam, as usual we gathered at Ritika's place and ate lunch prepared by her sweet mom. Afterwards we *Five Folks*[3] went out to watch a movie as we did at the end of the every academic year after the annual college exams ended.

Summer vacations had already started. Most of the students had gone home to see their parents. I also wanted to go home but in the meanwhile I found a sponsored course in Website Designing, sponsored by the Chemistry Department of the Hindu College, Delhi University. It was a good opportunity for me to learn how to design a website. At the end of the course I could have designed my own website if I joined this course. The idea of having my own website by the end of the summer vacation was very tempting so I dropped the idea of going home and instead joined the *'Institute for Computer Learning*[4]*'* for learning first of all how to operate a computer.

---

[3]   Five folks included Karishma, Meghna, Ritika, Sri Ram and me
[4]   A computer teaching centre,

At the Institute I learned how to operate MS Word and practiced typing on a computer keyboard. Simultaneously I had joined the Website Designing course. I picked up things fast and in a month I learned how to design a website and designed my own website as an assignment for the course by the end of the vacation.

Towards the end of the vacation I went home for a few days. My father was delighted to have me back home. When we met he told me -"I am proud of you my son". My mother was overjoyed to see me after a year. My relatives and neighbours flocked to see pictures of a foreign land that I had brought from Manila, Philippines.

Those precious words of my father will always be with me, during the time joy, during the times of distress. Rarely sons get such opportunities in their lives to make their fathers proud and happy and I was just eighteen when my father spoke those kind words to me. It is perhaps the best gift a son could give a father and this was perhaps the best gift I could give my father. I felt indebted to the supreme spiritual powers for blessing me with the gift to make my father happy.

I reminded my father of the words he had spoken to me when I was leaving home for Delhi. He had said- "Delhi is too far away my son and I would not be able to see you often" and I had replied- "Delhi is just overnight journey from here papa, what if I have to go to *America*[5] one day". My father smiled remembering those words, our eyes smiled together and we both knew how far we had come together in life.

I had not made it yet to the United States or to Europe for that matter but I had made it to Philippines in a very prestigious world event, representing my College, University and Country. It was a great leap forward for me, a young boy from the banks of the river Paimar, from the fact that my grandfather just three decades ago did not even go to the nearest school or the nearest town. I cannot say that every Indian has the same experience or every Indian has travelled the same distance but in the last three to five decades this is the distance an Indian family has travelled. My story is not every Indian's story but it is an Indian story.

---

[5]   America is considered to be a land of prosperity and riches somewhere far away

India is moving forward fast and my family is just one of many Indian families who are moving ahead with the progressive forces brought by a fast rising New India.

It had been a long time since I visited my grandpa last time. I visited my grandpa that summer. When I crossed the river Paimar I met him in the fields while he was happily grazing his cows. It took longer for his weak eyes to recognize me. When he was sure it's me he hugged me and I touched his feet as the young do when they meet their parents, grandparents or their teachers in this part of the world. Then we sat down on the bed of the green grass in the shadow of a mango tree and talked about the cows, sugarcanes, vegetables and of those sweet guavas and mangoes growing in abundance in grandma's orchards waiting for my return since long, since very long.... I had travelled miles away to the glittering cities and distant lands but this place; my birth place was the only place I felt completely at home...

Where one day I would like to finally rest,

When my journey on earth gets over

Amidst the mango grooves

Where the cuckoos sing the divine songs...

Under the shadow of the mango tree we discussed *Desh*[6], *Pardesh & Videsh*[7], and the lives of the foreigners who lived in distant lands. What did they eat, wear, what were their customs, religion, traditions etc. but most importantly whether did they have cows or not and what castes did they belong to? My grandpa found it strange that they did not have cows. He did not believe me when I told him the foreigners do not have caste system. He thought I was not well informed. Everybody must belong to some or the other caste.

Afterwards we walked slowly back to the village. He shouted with joy to every passer by and went shouting in every home in the village –"*mera pota aya hai, mera pota aya hai*"[8]. Soon the whole village gathered to see me. I showed them the photographs I had taken in Manila, Bangkok and Delhi and answered their questions about cows and castes. I stayed there for two days, met everybody in whose love and care I had grown up. I had missed them all for so long.

---

6   Home land
7   Pardesh and Videsh are used interchangeably meaning foreign land
8   My grandson has come, my grandson has come

At night I terribly missed my grandma. Earlier whenever I used to come here my grandma was always there for me. She told me stories and I slept holding her hand at night. Now she had long gone back to her eternal home. I missed her so much. For me she is still somewhere looking at me-'her little boy' from the stars or the moon...

Grandma you may be gone

But you live for me

In the shining sun

In the glowing moon

In the twinkling stars

In the blowing wind

In the falling rain

In the smell of the wet earth after the first rains

In the fairytales

In those ripened guavas in my and your orchard

In the sweetness of those sugarcanes

Which grow in the fields

Where I walked holding your little finger

In my thoughts of the most beautiful lady

Grandma you are always there

Your body may be gone

But you live in me

And my stories

Which I'll tell my children

And your great-grand children

I came back to my parents after staying two days with Grandpa. Chhabilapur had now turned into a modestly big village. My father had worked hard for many years to transform this place of a few hutments into a modern village. I must say he had been successful. It was a place where twenty years back there were only five odd huts but now it had more than hundred homes with total population of a more than thousand people. More than half of the houses were *'puccka*[9] 'houses. Chhabilapur now had a small but vibrant local market and a bus stand. Some homes even had television sets that run on battery power. District administration had set up a *thana*[10] on the request of the public of the area under

---

[9]   Made of brick
[10] A police station

the leadership of my father. It had a very positive influence on the law and order situation in Chhabilapur and the surrounding areas. Traders had started opening shops in the market place and the land prices had suddenly gone up. Especially land on the both sides of the road was in great demand among the new settlers to open shops. The village did not have telephone and electricity connection yet despite their many petitions to the district authorities. When I was in Chhabilapur I met the young people in the village and organized them to find solution to the problems the village was facing. Later we brought in the village elders to find a strategy to solve the telephone and electricity issue. They decided to go to the Block Development Officer and submit an application signed by everybody. Some differed and said "we should wait till the next State assembly elections. That time we can exchange our votes for telephone and *'bijli*[11]*'* connection". I decided to go to the district headquarter and meet the officials responsible for the electrification of the rural areas in the district. We met an executive engineer responsible for providing electricity to

---

[11]   Electricity

the villages. He said that work could be done in a month's time but the whole village should pay him thirty thousand rupees 'bribe' for it. We instantly left his place and informed the villagers about it. They decided to wait till the next state assembly elections.

My father was making his own efforts to get a telephone connection to Chhabilapur. He had applied to the district authorities for a pubic booth facility so that the common man could avail telephone facilities in the village. The district administration had been sitting on it since many months. When I went home I followed it up with the district officials and after many days of hard work I got the approval to open a telephone booth in the village.

After a very happy and purposeful stay at home I returned to Delhi reflecting how I had spent my last year. In essence my maximum energy during my second year at KM College was spent outside the classroom.

6

The Final Year

Then to the moment could I say

Linger you now, you are so fair

Now records of my earthly days

No flights of eons can impair

For knowledge comes and fills me with
such bliss

I take my joy, my highest moment this

- Goethe

I returned to Delhi very enriched and
happy after visiting my parents, my grandpa
and other relatives. Second Year Results had

already been published. After putting my luggage in the hostel I ran to see my results on the College notice-board. I had scored 65%. It was below the last year's score but not disappointing. The kind of preparation I had done for the second year annual exams I was expecting even less. I was satisfied with my result because my score was not too poor and I had many other achievements to my credit during my second year the College. Nevertheless I decided to improve it next year at least by 10-15% to maintain an average score of 70% as I had secured in the first year annual examination. The second year had opened a whole new world for me and I was truly "widening my horizons" as our teacher had once inspired me to do.

In the third year I was allotted a different room in the KM College hostel because my room mate Kamrul had already passed out. The hostel warden played politics on caste lines in allocation of the rooms so he favoured certain students over the other in allotting the better and spacious rooms in the hostel. I was given the similar kind of room in the same block as I had the last year. As each room had to be shared by two students after being allotted a room I was curious about who would be my room mate. One day a student knocked at my door while I was studying alone in the evening. He was from the north-east of India. He stood outside the door with his face lit up with a smile.

He asked me –"would you like to have me as your room-mate?"

I said smiling–"why not, with pleasure". His eyes lit up and face showed a sign of relief.

He said–"generally Indians do not like to live with us."

I was startled. I said–"you are an Indian too, why do you say so."

He told me that he had gone to other students and they did not like the idea of staying with a *Chinki*[1] He said–"they say that we eat dogs and look so different".

I said–"don't care about them and just shift in whenever you want."

His name was David. He was a third year student in the Political Science Department of the KM College. We became the best buddies

---

[1]   Slang used in North Campus for the students from the North-Eastern Indian states

after he shifted to the KM College hostel. We often went for a walk together in the evening. He played guitar like a professional and sang English songs with his melodious voice. He introduced me to altogether a different world of music and art which I had known very little about earlier. He enriched my life in so many ways, be it food or the books or the songs, he brought a completely fresh set of ideas that impressed me. He cared for the small yet very vital things in life, for example he always wished me "have a good day" whenever I left in the morning for the class and did never forget to ask "how was your day" at the end of the day. He always found a compliment or two for me for something or the other.

I really appreciate such things. A small compliment or two are not something that costs money but they do make us feel better about ourselves and the joy of living is multiplied several times. I have come across a very few people who really possess such rare qualities, who can make your day with a smile or a few kind words.

David had a very visible impact on my life. I started going to the Church with him just out of curiosity and found the Sunday mass interesting. He stood for something very gentle, soft, and humane and life felt like a smooth and gentle blow of breeze with him. It helped me to choose a career where gentleness and softness had more impact than brute force. The Foreign Service and Diplomacy came very close to that ideal career. I was already exposed to the enriching experience that any international gathering brought to one's life when I had met students from many different countries in Manila in 1998. In a way David helped me to consolidate my choice of becoming a career diplomat. When we passed out from Delhi University both of us joined JNU though in different schools but still we stayed in each other's company for another three years.

In the college I continued to participate in debates, social work and took active interest in the gender issues, nevertheless my main focus had shifted again to the studies and now I was more concerned about what I was going to do after the College. I wanted to take the Civil Services exam just after finishing the graduation course. For that I needed to study another optional subject besides Geography. I was thinking hard which subject to choose for the second optional paper for writing the Civil Services exam.

Civil Services exam is conducted by the Union Public Service Commission of India and is held in three phases. In the first phase which is called Preliminary Exam (Prelims in short) is an objective exam and consists of an optional paper and a paper of General Studies (GS). On an average a quarter of a million students sit for Prelims every year. Out of those only 3000-5000 students make it to the next stage of the Civil Services Exam. The next stage of the exam is called the "Mains". As the name suggests it is the main exam of Civil Services. It is a marathon if one would like to call the prelims a sprint. "Mains" consists of two optional papers, the papers one can choose, a paper of general studies, a separate paper of essay, a paper of the English language and a paper of Hindi or any one of the specified national languages of India. The marks obtained in the English language and Hindi or other language papers do not add up to the sum total of marks obtained in Mains exam but failing to pass in these two language papers leads to disqualification of the candidate from the Civil Services Exam. On an average 800-1000 students make it to the third phase of the exam which is called "Interview". In interview the candidates are personally examined by a group of very experienced people in different walks of life. Generally only 300 to 400 candidates make it finally to the list of the successful candidates. Then they undergo through a medical test. Only after it is proved beyond doubt that candidate is free from any serious medical problems he is given the final green signal and becomes a probationer in the Indian Civil Service.

All these requirements make Indian Civil Service exam as one of the toughest and most challenging exams to pass in the whole world. Prior planning and hard work is required to be successful in this mother of all exams. I had decided to keep Geography as one of the optional papers as I was studying it at the College but it was very difficult to choose the other optional paper. During this course I met *Rajesh Bhaiya* who had been preparing with Geography and Psychology as his optional papers since the past many years. He showed me his notes and encouraged me to take Psychology as my second optional for the Civil Services Mains exam. I was not very sure about it but seeing that it was both science and arts and was as *scoring* [2] as Geography, helped me to consolidate my decision. It took me another few months to finally make up my mind to take up Psychology as my second optional for the Mains exam. I also made up my mind to join a coaching institute to study Psychology just after passing out my final year exams.

An important development during that time was arrival of Dr. Avinash to Delhi. I knew him since my days in Patna. He was nephew of the Chemistry Reader at whose place I lived as a paying guest. He was preparing for Civil Services exam since a long time along with doing his medical internship in Nalanda Medical College and Hospital in Patna. Now he had got a job at a government hospital in old Delhi and had come to live in Delhi. He had already passed the Preliminary exam and was preparing to write Civil Services Mains exam. He was looking for a study-partner. Since I was perhaps the only person he knew in Delhi he asked me to study with him. I agreed to study with him and thus began my journey

[2]   A paper in which on can easily score compared to some other papers in which it is slightly difficult to score even after performing well in the exam

into the Civil Services world. I began, for the first time to study seriously Indian history, science & technology, culture, politics, economics, art, architecture etc. We used to do past year papers of the Civil Services Mains exam together. My job was to write answers of the questions asked in the previous years of Mains exam looking into the books, magazines or anywhere I could find. I just had to find and write the answers. This proved very useful to me later when I started studying General Studies on my own. I already knew where to look for the answers and what kinds of questions were expected. This also provided me with a very important insight into how to handle the exam well which I applied in other papers as well. It was the insight to go after the questions and not to waste one's time in studying specific books suggested by the Civil Services Gurus. Once I was sure what kind of questions were expected and how to answer them, books became just sources to find the answers. It was not necessary anymore to read the whole book and then grasp its meaning and what was it all about. Now I could cover more topics in less time by adopting a question-centric approach. My principle was –"Read as much as you need", especially for highly competitive Civil Services exam. Thus in a short time I had started feeling comfortable about taking the 'exam of my life'. The only big hurdle was to master a completely new subject "Psychology".

My elder brother was still in Biharshariff. He was doing a degree course in Chemistry from *Kishan College*[3], *Magadh University*[4] since the past many years but had not completed it yet. The reason was that he hardly studied Chemistry. His main goal was to join any bank in India as a bank clerk. He thought this is the only job he could get very quickly as his other friends and acquaintances had got. He was trying his best to get that job since 1992. He had spent prime time of his life in pursuit of his dream to become a bank clerk but so far had not tasted the fruits of success. I really admired his patience and perseverance but I thought he should do something else if things were not working out for him in the banking field. I had asked him many times to come to Delhi and start something new. He hardly

---

[3]   College named after farmers
[4]   One of the largest universities of India located in Bihar

listened to me as he wanted to stay close to parents at home.

When I had gone home for the summer vacation last time I somehow persuaded him to prepare for his graduation degree exam and to write it. He listened to me for the first time and passed it. After graduating in Chemistry after eight years of study he came to Delhi to stay with me while I was a final year student at the KM College. I found together a place for him not very far from the College hostel as he could not stay with me in the hostel as per the rules. I suggested him to do some basic computer course which could get him a job in a year or two but his heart was still in the bank. Now he had a graduation degree so he started preparing for the bank Probationary Officer (PO) exam. The reason he could not finally pass most of the exams was his very weak English language skills. He started working seriously on his English for the first time after coming to Delhi. He carried on with his efforts to improve his English and I carried on with my preparation for Civil Services Exam along with preparing for my final year college exams. We met once or twice in a week; I encouraged him to converse in English, he used to hesitate in the beginning but later on he started making slow progress.

During this time the Geography Department of the KM College decided to take the final year students for an excursion to South India. It was a welcome surprise as the last year students had gone to Bhutan and the department largely focused on North India. It was an opportunity for me to see the South of my country for the first time. I was excited. We took a train to *Ernakulam*[5] from Nijjamudin Railway station, Delhi. The journey lasted for good 36 hours. It took us through the beautiful country side passing through the ravines and badlands of *Chambal*[6], *Deccan plateau*[7], the tunnels in the undulating hills of the *Western Ghats*[8], and the coastal plains crossing many rivers. 'The beauty of Kerala -'*God's Own Country*', as Keralites and outsiders often like to call it, is beyond words. Coconut trees grow in abundance amidst the green rice fields along the sea shore in the hilly countryside. Valleys

---

[5] A coastal city in state of Kerala
[6] Badlands in the state of Madhya Pradesh
[7] A lava plateau spread over the states of Maharashtra and Karnataka
[8] Low lying hills along the western coast of India

full of clouds and hills with tea plantations and spice plants give the whole place an enchanted look.

Our accommodation had been arranged near a print-paper manufacturing factory not very far away from the city of Cochin. We saw the scenic beauty of *Munnar*[9], visited tea plantations and the hills where spices grew. We went for a boat ride in the coastal backwaters near Cochin. The boat-ride in the backwaters proved to be adventurous and scary as a big wave threw many of us off the board. Somehow we managed to catch the railing and got saved. In Cochin for the first time in my life I visited a Synagogue, a place of worship for the Jews. I instantly felt the vastness and greatness of India, a land where people belonging to diverse communities, religions, faiths and opinions lived together in harmony since centuries, respecting and learning from each other.

After spending two days in Kerala we went to Bangalore, the Silicon Valley of India and one of the leading global centres of *R&D*[10]. We

---

[9]   A scenic hill station in the state of Kerala
[10] Research and Development

conducted a survey of the transport routes of the congested city to get some geographical information about the city's traffic. 'It's a beautiful city with a huge green area and that's why I think, it is called garden city of India.' We had a pleasant boat ride in the Ulsoor Lake near the city centre, visited the Indian Science Centre and the Tippu Sultan[11] Museum. At night some of my classmates decided to go to a pub. So we went to the down town. Pubs and the cyber cafes were mushrooming fast in those days in this city and we tasted a slice of *Banglorean* life. After a day we visited Mysore. 'It is a very beautiful city, not very far away from Bangalore. It has palaces and beautiful gardens with fountains. The Krishna Raja Sagar dam is located here. It is a beautiful example of Indian engineering. It was built in 1924 by Sir M. Vishveswariah, one of India's finest engineers. After visiting Mysore we returned to Bangalore and took a train back to Delhi, again passing trough the beautiful country side showing the huge geographical diversity of India.

---

[11] A visionary warrior and a strategic military planner and innovator of the world's first war rocket, also known as the "Tiger of Mysore"

Time passed by fast. Final year exam was nearing and the college life was coming to an end. Ritika was still around but I had the sinking feeling at times that soon we shall part and we would not see each other everyday, those annual outings after the exam would end and my inspiration would be gone for ever-

Whose face will I look at in the morning?

Whose voice will touch my heart?

Whose eyes will I enter into and

Whose giggles will fill my mind?

Whose smile will bring a smile on my face?

Whose words will motivate me?

Whose actions will speak loud-"go on"

Whose examples will I follow?

While I am down and out

Whose, whose, whose...?

If not hers?

Our juniors in the Geography Department organized a farewell party for the final year students who were soon going to pass out. Everyone came formally dressed and everyone had something to say as the occasion was an emotional one for each one of us. Girls wore beautiful saris while boys were dressed in suits. I had my own little farewell speech in which I had tried to sum up my feelings during the last three years I had spent in the KM College. I thanked everybody for being good and helpful to me. I specially acknowledged the inspiration I had found in the Geography Department and the opportunities I had got in the College. I thanked my teachers for their guidance and motivation and always being patient with my tricky questions. I thanked the non teaching members of the Geography department for their support in organizing picnics, excursions and for keeping our classrooms clean and beautiful. Some among them said deep and remarkable words which would always remain with me. We were given mementos by Shri Bhimsen Singh, the Principal of the College, to remember the wonderful days we had spent in the College. That day everyone clicked pictures with each other just to remember by a beautiful part of one's life. It was one of the difficult days. We were happy that a whole new world was going to open to us and sad because we would not see each other any more and our friends would head in different directions pursuing life wherever it takes them.

Final year exam was at the doorstep. Almost everybody was rushing to the library reading room once again. I was at complete ease this year. Exam did not bother me at all as I had studied well the whole year. Exam went on smoothly. We, the Five Folks, met in the afternoon after the last exam and repeated the ritual of going first to Ritika's place for lunch and then out to watch a movie. We all were conscious of the fact that it was the last time we were going out for a movie together. I do not remember which movie did we watch but it was a great feeling to be together once again doing the things we always did when exams got over. We parted for the summer holidays once again but this time no one was really sure that whether we shall meet again or not. I had my career in my mind so I used this time to study Psychology, my second optional paper for the Civil Services Exam. I joined the coaching classes for Psychology that offered to help me master the subject just in three months. I took it easy and just believed in what people at the coaching institute said. Later it proved fatal for me when I lost one precious year just because I took a completely new subject for granted.

Summer holidays got over and results were declared. The summer of 2000 brought cheers on my face once again. I had scored well over seventy five percent marks in the final year exam and thus my aggregate average for the three years had become seventy percent. This was very pleasing indeed and an important step towards a better future. Now a very important question squarely looked into my face. Should I do post-graduation or just prepare for the Civil Services exam? I also had to choose between JNU[12] and DSE[13] if I decided to do post-graduation. I was still twenty and therefore even after passing graduation I could not sit for the Civil-Services exam as the minimum age for sitting in this exam was twenty one years. My colleagues, parents and teachers advised me to first complete post-graduation and then take the Civil-Services exam. I thought there was no harm in taking admission but I decided to write the exam in the middle of the course after one year without completing post graduation. Now I had to make a choice between the DSE and JNU. My

---

[12] Jawaharlal Nehru University
[13] Delhi School of Economics

father was very keen that I should study in JNU while most of my friends took admission in DSE including Ritika. I was worried to go away from my source of inspiration but ultimately my father prevailed upon me and I took admission in JNU.

7

Jawaharlal Nehru University

Where mind is without fear and the head
is held high

Where knowledge is free

Where the world is not broken into
fragments by narrow domestic walls...

Where words come from depth of truth

Where tireless striving stretches its arms
towards perfection

Where clear stream of reason has not lost
its way into dreary desert sand
of dead habit

-Gitanjali, Rabindranath Tagore

Jawaharlal Nehru University (JNU) is the leading University of India and one of the best in Asia. It has students from all over India and many Asian and African and East European countries. To enter JNU one has to pass a very tough competitive examination on a national level. This university has established many Centres of Excellence over the years. The CSRD[1] is one of them. I was admitted to CSRD in August 2000. I was not the only one from KM College to get admitted in CSRD. My classmate *Meghna*[2] had also made it to JNU. Meghna was part of the Five Folks who went out every year after the KM College annual exams. She had been always there in the group but I did not notice her much. It was towards the end of the third year when we did the Cartographical Survey together, we got to know each other well for the first time. She had missed the Survey report submission deadline like me and we had to meet the second submission deadline. So we decided to do it together. It took the full day and that day we had lunch together. Then we met again when our final year exams at the College ended and we 'Five

---

[1]   Center for the Study of Regional Development
[2]   My classmate at KM College from Dibrugarh, Assam

Folks' went out for a movie. After that we parted for the summer vacation. We met again when almost all the passed out students from the KM College Geography Department gathered in the campus of Delhi School of Economics (DSE) to write the entrance exam for the DSE.

That day Meghna asked me "where would you like to study... at JNU or DSE?"

I said looking away from her -"I don't know, haven't decided yet".

I wanted to be in DSE with Ritika because she had been a good friend and a source for inspiration for me since last three years. I really hated the fact that she had not made it to JNU.

I had shifted out of the KM College hostel to a flat in Kamla Nagar after passing out from the KM College. Meghna took my address and phone number from Ritika and managed to find out my flat in Kamlanagar. She came to see me one day while I was away attending Psychology classes in the coaching institute. She left a message for me and her phone number so that I could call her back.

I was not sure what to do. I had not made

up my mind yet to go to JNU. My father somehow had found out that JNU is the best place to study in India and had advised me to take admission there. Now Meghna also wanted a company to travel from North Delhi to South Delhi where JNU was located. She was just looking for a travel-partner. I wanted to give it a try so I called her up and told her that I would try out some classes in JNU and see whether I would like it there or not.

We used to take an auto-rickshaw from the Kamlanagar to Connaught Place. There we waited for sometime everyday for the bus number six hundred fifteen at the *Kasturba Gandhi Marg*[3] to go to the JNU campus. It took an hour by bus to reach the main campus from there. I enjoyed the bus ride even though it used to be very crowded during the day.

I remember the first day at JNU in the class. Everybody looked at two of us. We giggled and ran out of the class. There was something very funny in the way our new classmates at CSRD looked at us. Soon I found the classes boring and a repetition of what we had already learned at the KM College therefore after a

---

[3]   The old Curzon Road

few classes I decided to leave JNU. At the same time I also thought that there was no need to do Masters because it would have taken a lot of my quality time away from the preparation of the Civil Services exam. But there were other attractions. I liked the JNU campus so much in just a few days that I had to rethink my decision to leave JNU. I wanted to live somewhere very close to the JNU campus.

'JNU is a world in itself. It has a beautiful campus isolated from the rest of the city. The campus is located on a hilly terrain in the south of Delhi. The terrain being an extension of the *Aravali*[4] *hills* is home to many species of plants and animals. The campus is extremely beautiful and looks as if this place was just created for this University. It has some kind of magical influence on the new entrants who suddenly turn to a new dress code–mainly *kurta-pajama*[5] and *chappals*[6], and take an ideological leaning to the left. JNU is known as the bastion of the

---

[4] Low lying hills extending from the south of Delhi down to the western states of India Haryana, Rajasthan & Gujarat

[5] A loose long cotton dress worn in summer in South Asia

[6] Slippers

left and to an extent this image has stayed on the campus since the day it was founded. Since that time in the annual student presidential elections the left parties have been dominating. A sub-culture has evolved within the campus over the years. It enriches the lives of the new-comers and in turn it gets enriched by the experiences brought by the students from the different regions, cultures, religions and societies who join the mainstream of JNU. It has many residential hostels where students from the different parts of the country live and study. The campus has many *Dhabas* that serve tea, snacks and other necessities of the students at subsidized rates. One of the *Dhabas* named after the river Ganges 'Ganga *dhaba*' is very popular among the students inside as well as outside the JNU campus. It is a symbol of the JNU sub-culture as is the bus number 615 which links the main city from the campus. Thus from the ideological leaning to the dress code and the means of transport and places to eat, JNU stands apart from the rest of the Universities in India. In the terms of gender equality and liberty the campus is the most liberal in the country. It has the hostels where the boys and the girls live and dine together. There is no restriction on the movement of the students anywhere and anytime in the campus except that boys can't enter the girl's hostel while girls can come to boy's hostel.'

In these settings I joined JNU in the late August of the year 2000, the School of Social Sciences in the Centre for the Study of Regional Development (CSRD) for a Master of Arts degree in Geography. I had joined this course with the hope that it will allow me enough time to study for my Civil Services exam but on the contrary it hardly gave me time even to recreate. I decided to leave the course and straight away prepare for the competitive exam. I knew that I would face the problem of accommodation if I left JNU. Now I was in a dilemma. I had to think something fast as time was running out. I looked for some options to live outside the campus but it created new problems- the problem of heavy monthly rent and food. JNU hostels at least ensured that I could manage in just Rupees1000 (~$20) per month and food was taken care by the hostel mess. I decided to stay in the campus, do the course and prepare for the Civil Services exam at the same time. How could I do that in the limited time I had? I made myself very focused.

I did not need a MA degree but I needed the hostel so I continued in the course but just on the fringes while I found the right kind of people to prepare for the exam.

One day I was walking in the campus when I met *Girijesh*[7], who had been preparing for this exam since a number of years and was my classmate at CSRD but he hardly attended any classes. We met, spoke for a while, our wavelengths matched and we teamed up to prepare for the challenging Civil Services exam. He was an early riser and a very health conscious person. We lived in different hostels. Initially we only met after the dinner for an hour everyday just to revise the maps and the geographical locations of the world but slowly we started expanding the areas of joint study and even the time we spent together. Gradually it became round the clock business. We ate, slept and dreamed Geography. Those days literally lived in his room and only came to my hostel to take a shower and to eat lunch and dinner. He got up early in the morning and went for a jog, took a shower and got ready for the day while I slept. When I used to get

---

[7]   An engineer from Uttranchal

up, my breakfast used to be already on the table and Girijesh into the books. I used to join him then and we studied together till the lunch time. After the lunch we took a short nap and afterwards study continued even during we drank tea at the *Sabarmati Dhaba*[8] in the evening. We decided not to waste a single minute so when we went to *Dhaba* for *chai*[9] and *pakora*[10], we carried the notes and revised the things we had learnt. We always carried a packet of Glucose with us. It was our instant energy supplier. We went out at nights in the open when we got really suffocated studying in the four walls of the room and studied under the street lamps. Sometimes passers by laughed at us.   It was fun to study this way as we never got bored studying. Later we decided even to use the time we spent during walking or travelling in the *auto*[11] or the bus. We recorded the facts related to History, Geography, Polity, Economics etc. in blank cassettes and listened to them while walking

---

[8] A snacks& tea stall in front of the Sabarmati girls & boys hostel in JNU

[9] Tea

[10] Evening snacks made of wheat flour and deep fried in oil

[11] Auto-rickshaw

from the hostel to the classroom or when we went out for a walk in the evening. I bought a walkman for this purpose, Girijesh already had one, so he just helped me to buy one. Girijesh had a *Bullet*[12] motorbike. Whenever we went out we carried our walkmans and wore earphones. People thought that we had just gone crazy as they thought we kept on listening to rock and pop music all the time. I used to wear *Pink Floyd*[13] T-shirts those days and perhaps that further added on some spice to their imagination. We worked this way for three months till the Preliminary exam. The exam went well and we were satisfied by our performance.

The next day I had to leave on an excursion to the Himalayas for 10 days. It was a great break but I carried the *IGNOU*[14] History books to the tents in the high Himalayas and at night when everybody went off to sleep I read them under the torch light. I really enjoyed doing that and I read all the books I was carrying during the excursion. At the First day we

---

[12] Enfield motorbike that makes a lot of noise while riding
[13] A popular band of psychedelic music
[14] Indira Gandhi National Open University

camped at *Uttarakashi*[15] and the next day we moved high up in the Himalayas to our destination *Gomukh*[16] glacier after trekking for more than fourteen kilometres. Our assignment was to measure the recession of the *Gomukh* glacier under the leadership of Professor Milapchand Sharma and to study the effects of global warming on the Himalayan glaciers. The weather conditions in the high Himalayas are completely different from the North Indian plains and for most of us it was a life time experience to be there. We returned to JNU very satisfied and enriched.

Mains were always in my mind so even after the Prelim exam we did not stop working because it had become the way of life for us. There was no fun outside it which we knew. We just changed the content but kept the style. Now the requirements were different and we needed someone else who had the experience of writing the Civil Services Mains exam. We found the third study partner without many difficulties. He was our classmate in CSRD and had written the Mains exam a number of times

---

[15] A town in the Himalayan state of Uttranchal
[16] The place from where the Ganges originate

but without success. He was trying his luck again. We decided to learn from his experience and knowledge about this exam. He was also keen to study together and we formed a new team. We did not change our style. His name was Ajay. He adjusted well to our ways though he was used to study alone. Days passed by fast and we kept our pace. By the end of the preparation time we were comfortable in Geography as well as in the General Studies.

I had to look for a different study partner for Psychology. It was difficult to find one but I tried my best and found a senior from the CSRD who was planning to take the exam the next year. He turned out to be very helpful as studying with him helped me to improve my knowledge of the subject. Nevertheless I did not feel very comfortable yet in Psychology. Three of us wrote the exam at different centres in Delhi. Overall it turned out to be good and I expected to get a call for the Civil Service Interview but I was not too sure because after all it was a competition. The team disbanded for a while after the exam and we did different things.

I was not doing too well in the term papers I wrote for the CSRD and my grades in the

M.A. Geography classes were falling gradually. It was quite demoralizing not to be one of the best but I had no other option. I accepted my limitations and accepted that I could not do many things at the same time. My main focus was the Civil Services exam and I was happy with my preparation.

I sat and did some 'so what' self-talking for a while-

"I am not a favourite of my professors."

"So what?"

I was not meant to be their favourite anyway.

I went to the library just once or twice in the whole semester"

"So what?"

I never wanted to be a Geographer or a research scholar anyway.

In JNU I had discovered a new way of life that was very different from the way I lived in Delhi University. I had discovered the campus of JNU with my College time friend David. I used to borrow his bicycle sometimes to take a ride in the JNU campus. I had gifted my guitar to David. He carried it everywhere. He carried it to the bonfires in the cold nights where he sang Bob Dylan and Bob Marley at one stretch and around the ring road inside the JNU at moon-lit nights when he played soft soothing love songs while we walked. Sometimes together we visited *Boss*, not a real boss but a common friend who lived just outside the campus. Boss had a great sense of humour and he always made us laugh. He made good tea. David often played some of the Boss's favourite songs after he came out of the kitchen after making tea for us. *Stephan*[17] lived not very far away from Boss's flat and we were often invited to his place for special North-East Indian dinner. Stephan was the eldest and the most experienced among all of us. We called him "the Rock". He was to be immediately consulted if anybody had a problem with the heart, not the cardiological problems but the emotional ones. He was an expert in the matters of heartbreaks and unanswered crushes; the only problem was that he took them too seriously. I joined David, Boss and Stephan in the Church sometimes for a service on Sundays. I liked the ambience there. Afterwards we always had

---

[17]   Another friend of David who had been preparing for Civil Services

lunch together in *Teflas*[18], JNU. We spent the afternoons chatting or just walked around in the beautiful JNU campus. In the evenings I usually met Stephan in the stadium where he came regularly. He exercised to shed a few extra kilos while I ran a few rounds to keep myself fit.

The results of the Mains exam were to be declared in a month's time and the pressure had started building up to prepare for the Interview in case I got through Mains exam or for the Preliminaries in case I did not get through. In any case I had to tighten up my life once again and get into the thick of the things. I started myself this time and a few other classmates joined me gradually. I took things a little easy and I was almost sure that I was going to make it. Mains results were out. I was in. I was not surprised but I was really happy to make it in the first attempt in this marathon of exams. At the same time there was some bad news, my team-mates Girijesh and Ajay had not been lucky enough to make it through the Mains. My team was broken. Without their help and support I could not have moved even an inch. The reality was

18 A canteen in JNU, strangely no one knew why was it called Teflas

staring straight in my face. I carried on my
own for a while but ultimately I had to
painfully search for some like minded study
partners. I did find them but I really missed
not studying with Girijesh and Ajay. It was so
much fun to study together with them.

Interview is another milestone one has to
cross before reaching the destination. I prepared
questions on my family and educational
background, the district and the state I belonged
to, the subjects I had studied in the school, the
College and the University and the optional
papers I had chosen for the Civil Services exam,
the preference of the services I wanted to join,
why the Foreign Service was my first choice
etc. The list was large and the time was short.
There was the danger that if I could not make
it finally I had to take Preliminary exam again
and this time without any preparation as the
final results came out just two or three days
before the day of the preliminary exam. To
add on to my difficulties the *M.Phil*[19] entrance
exam was just a day before the day of the
Preliminary exam. I was under tremendous
pressure to perform well under all

---

[19]   Master of Philosophy

circumstances because I had no other choice. It was a "do or die" situation. I walked alone at nights for hours on the roads of JNU brooding over the questions and answers for the interview. More I thought about the questions more clarity came to my answers.

Finally the D-Day came. It was summer and the campus was burning bright with the red and yellow flowers. I went for the Interview wearing a sky blue shirt, light blue colour neck tie and the charcoal suit that I had got stitched before going to the World Debates in Manila in 1998. My interview was in the first half of the day. I took an auto in the morning from JNU and reached *Dholpur house*, the venue for Civil Services interview. I was allocated to an interview board headed by *Shri TK Madan*.

When I entered the interview room I was nervous and the board members tried to make me comfortable. I am not sure they were very successful because the questions they asked really unsettled me. Most of the questions were objective in nature and mainly sought for one line information. I could not answer most of them. They did not ask many opinion based questions. I was far from satisfied with my interview.

I returned to JNU and concentrated on the M.Phil. entrance exam. It was the most important thing in front of me at that point if I wanted to stay in the JNU campus any longer.

My elder brother by now was a student of JNU. He had shifted near the JNU campus to stay close to me when I had moved from the Delhi University to JNU. He too had fallen in love with JNU campus like me. He had met JNU students and made some new friends. I had advised him to learn a foreign language in JNU and leave the preparation for a career in banks for the good. He liked the first part but not the second one. He still wanted to work in a bank. I advised him to do a degree course in a foreign language. For this he had to write the competitive entrance exam for JNU. He had a tough challenge to face because only very few seats were available for the students who were not fresh pass-outs from the Senior Secondary Schools. He prepared for this exam well and managed to get admission in JNU for the degree course in the Spanish language.

When I completed my M.A. in Geography from CSRD, JNU he was already in the second year of the degree course at the School of languages. He was always around. We usually met in the evening everyday and I encouraged him to converse in English with me so that he could improve his foreign language skills. He was regular at JNU Yoga centre and had learned Yoga fast. He was improving day by day. I was surprised with the pace he was transforming himself. Now he could do translations from English to Spanish and vice-versa. He had left preparing for the banks for a while and was concentrating on his Spanish language skills. Now he confidently talked about his seniors who had joined the multi-national companies with fat salaries. He was looking forward himself to join one of these global giants within a few years after passing out from JNU.

It was a welcome surprise for me as so far the best paid jobs in India used to be jobs of Civil Servant, a doctor, a lawyer or an engineer. It seemed to me that time had changed for good. For a while I thought even I should learn Spanish in JNU and join a multi-national company after passing out from the Schools of Languages but I was already into the deep waters of Civil Services that it was difficult to come out of it and so I carried on with preparation for Civil Services Exam .

The long wait was over the final results of the Civil Services exam had been declared. I rushed to the nearest cyber café to check the results. Sadly I had not made it to the list of the successful candidates. It was a great shock for me. I had to write the M.Phil. entrance exam in just two days time and Civil Services Prelims on the third day. Suddenly I found myself under a very stressful situation and decided to take a break from the preparation of Civil Services for a year. My brother was my only support in those trying times. It was my brother who motivated me and made all efforts he could to take me to the examination centre. There he stayed outside waiting the whole day while I took the Prelims once again. He was a great support during that difficult phase. If he were not around I would have been writing a very different story in some very different part of the world.

8

An Accident &
Opportunity

And that inverted Bowl we call the sky
Where under crawling coop't
We live and die
Lift not thy hands to it for help
For it rolls impotently on as thou or I
-Rubaiyat, Omar Khayam

My Prelims exam had not gone very well
and I was not very sure about making it to
Mains this time. Anyway I waited for the details
of the final results so that I could analyze my

failure in the last Civil Services Exam. Meanwhile I had to handle stress as too many things were happening at the same time. Earlier I had learned Transcendental Meditation™ along with Girijesh when we together prepared for the Mains exam in 2001. Now I had a lot of free time so I meditated for an hour everyday. I also went for jogging and played football in the evening. One of these days I was very upset with something and while playing football that evening I hurt myself. I was trying to defend a goal and the player from the opposite side hit me at my right knee accidentally. As a result I could not move afterwards. My brother was also playing with me that evening and with the help of others he managed to take me to the hostel. An ambulance was called immediately and I was taken to the *Safdarjang Medical College & Hospital*[1]. An X-ray was immediately done. X-ray report showed a hairline fracture in my right knee. I was sure it would get alright in sometime but doctors had something else to say. They plastered my leg and ordered six weeks compulsory bed rest. It was yet another

---

[1]   A hospital located in South Delhi

shock for me besides not finally getting through the Civil Services exam.

I had never been in bed in my life earlier even for a week and now six weeks mandatory bed rest was too much to bear. I was crumbling from inside and felt helpless. This accident added to my stress and I started losing my temper very quickly. At this point of time I received the details of the result of final exam of Civil Services 2002. I found I had done well in Geography and General Studies but had performed badly in Psychology. In fact my scores were unexpectedly low in this paper. At once I decided to put in more efforts in studying Psychology starting from that moment, even during the mandatory bed rest. Because of the bed rest I got more time to study and could concentrate better. Every thing I needed, my brother got them in my bed. I felt peaceful. In those difficult times I developed some spiritual insights. A strange kind of calmness and peace descended on me at times that I had never experienced or felt before in my life and have never felt till today since the day I got out of the mandatory bed rest. Only strong memories or emotions bring back that kind of feeling but never like the one had I felt during those days.

In a short time my pace of learning improved and I started feeling at ease in Psychology. Thus I had converted my accident into an opportunity.

In the meanwhile Prelims results had been declared while my right leg was still plastered. I had made it to Civil Services Mains once again. Tears rolled out of my eyes. I felt one with the universe at that moment. That time I had an intuition that nothing could stop me from finally getting what I wanted. I asked everybody to leave me alone for a while. All my fears and stress were washed away with those tears. I celebrated my success silently and worked even harder since the next day. I remained in the bed for another few weeks. I had developed a kind of liking for it.

After two weeks when I was taken out of the hostel to the hospital to change the plaster I saw the outside world from the ambulance and found it to be very fresh. Everything looked new. I envied people who could walk. Walking seemed to me such a great luxury. I thought for a while how good it would be to walk once again! During those days my elder brother was always with me. He brought me food, took me to the toilet with the help of some floor-mates and got me new books to read. Without him perhaps I could not have had the good time I had during those six weeks of bed rest.

After six weeks when my plaster was cut I thought I could walk instantly, but I was mistaken. I could not move an inch. My plastered leg had grown weaker during those six weeks in bed. I could not even bend it. The doctor told me to regularly exercise my right leg for a week along with putting ointments two times a day. So I had to continue in the bed rest even after the compulsory six weeks bed rest was over. I had no other choice. I exercised regularly and waited for that moment I could again start walking.

The results of the JNU M.Phil. entrance exam had been declared while I was still in bed and happily I had unexpectedly topped it. It was a wonderful surprise for me as well as for others as I was not expecting even to get through this difficult entrance exam. I had consistently received bad grades during the four semesters of M.A. (Geography) in CSRD. I had unintentionally rubbed many of the Professors at the Centre on the wrong side. I was sure that even if I managed to get good marks in the written exam the Professors would give me low marks in the M.Phil. viva exam. Therefore getting through the M.Phil. entrance exam was almost impossible for me. So when I heard that I had topped it, in fact I was shocked.

Even after completing M.A. (Geography) from CSRD I was staying in Narmada hostel with a special permission of the Dean of Students of JNU, *Professor Qureshi* who taught in CSRD and personally knew me. My health condition did not allow me to leave the hostel yet therefore I stayed for another week in the same hostel. My brother helped me to exercise properly and massaged my leg with ointment everyday. Finally I started walking, first with his help with a crutch and later on my own. My brother completed the admission formalities for me as I was in the bed and got a new hostel allotted for me. I had already exceeded the allowed duration of my stay in the present *Narmada*[2] Hostel.

I shifted to a new hostel after a week. It was named after the Sutlaj River. I had a new roommate. His name was Avinash. He never looked around while studying if anyone entered the room rather he put all his concentration in

[2]   A river in central part of India, most of the JNU hostels are named after the names of the Indian rivers

his books. It was strange for me because I had never studied like that. In the evening his girlfriend came to visit him at a fixed time and they laughed together exactly for half an hour and then suddenly everything turned silent. He went back into his books again and never looked left or right. I preferred group study and could not study alone like Avinash. I had lost my team long time back and there was no chance to revive it. Girijesh had not been able to make it to the Prelims this time. Ajay had made it but he wanted to study alone like Avinash. I was too on my own this time, studying alone. There was no fun in it but I had no other choice but to carry on my own. I had developed the habit of studying Psychology alone when I was in bed rest for more than six weeks. This habit helped me to cope with the new challenges I had ahead of me.

Those days I faced financial problems as I did not feel good asking money from my father anymore. Although I knew he would never say no if I asked for money. I guess it was changing times that made me uncomfortable asking money from my father any longer. I felt grown up I wanted to earn my own money rather than asking from my father. Therefore I decided to find a job for myself. I thought to give take a chance in the booming *outsourcing*[3] business industry in India. This non-traditional sector offered a great opportunity to the freshly passed out graduates from the different Universities of India. A generation earlier a student with a graduate or postgraduate degree in India could only think of entering the traditional careers viz. law, teaching, medicine, engineering etc. with terrible salaries to begin with. Now the *call centres* [4] offered a great start with start-up salaries that my father and his generation could only dream of a generation back. Now the fresh graduates just out of the University could make good money working in a call centre in the big metropolitan cities of India.

I was too tempted to start earning myself as soon as possible so I went for a few Interviews for the call centre jobs in *Gurgaon*[5],

---

[3]   The process of getting cheaper services taking the advantage of cheap well trained labour force in a different geographical location

[4]   Center for the outsourcing business

[5]   A fast growing suburb around Delhi, where most of the call centers are located

NOIDA[6] and in Delhi. I appeared in a few interviews but I got rejected at the first instance in all them. Probably my accent was not Americanized enough. I had lost the only window of opportunity I had to earn my own money and support my studies. Perhaps this is true for a million of Indian students who graduate from thousands of Colleges across India and find no window of opportunity to start a life by earning themselves. The opportunities for the students who study in the *Convent*[7] schools or the Private schools are many, including the Call Centre jobs but what is in store ahead for the students passing out from the millions of the Government run vernacular medium schools?

I met failures after failures and they scared me. During those trying times I looked towards the mushrooming *'coaching institute industry*[8]*'* with hope to get an opportunity to teach Geography in any of the institutes. I had scored

---

6 Abbreviation of New Okhla Institutional Development Authority but now this name is used for a fast growing suburb near Delhi

7 Schools run by the Christian Missionaries

8 Coaching centers for the civil services exam, a mushrooming industry those days in Delhi

well in the last Civil Services Mains exam in Geography paper and I was confident that I could teach Geography to the Civil Service aspirants. In the Hindu national daily I saw an advertisement of a coaching institute called **IDP3**. I thought they were new so they might need someone to teach Geography there. Geography was one of the most popular subjects among Civil Services aspirants and every coaching institute in the city offered its students coaching in this popular subject. So I called them up to find out if they needed a Geography coach. IDP3 had a lady director. She spoke on the phone –"you may come to see me tomorrow evening, please bring your mark-sheet of the last Mains exam along with you. You sound young. How old are you?"

I said -"I am twenty-two, Madam".

She said "you are too young to teach as most of our students are older than you but come anyway."

Next day I was there, sitting in front of her in the evening after a fifteen minute walk from my hostel in JNU. She asked-"Why do want to teach?"

I said- "because I have to revise my own

subject and I need to earn money to support my studies"

She further asked-"don't your parents support your studies?"

I said -"yes they do but I need to earn my own money. I feel grown up to ask money from my parents."

She said-"you are too young. Many of my students whom you will teach are older than you. How will you manage to teach them?"

I said- "Madam, I know my age matters but more than that what matters is my ability to help them learn Geography. Please give me a chance. Let me take one class of Geography. If students find it good and are satisfied then I would be very happy to continue."

She said-"alright you have a chance then. Go ahead. Please come tomorrow evening prepared in any area of your choice in Geography and we'll see then."

I thanked her for giving me the opportunity and came back to JNU. I prepared a topic in Human Geography and went to the IDP3 the next evening. In the classroom I found many faces, young men and women in their twenties.

I felt a bit nervous but soon I got back my calm and composure when I started interacting with them. I introduced myself putting emphasis on my score in Geography in the last Civil Services Mains exam. Some faces became more curious and they asked several questions related to the preliminary and mains exam of the Civil Services. I was a source of first hand information for them. They had other teachers but no one had come straight to teach after just writing the Civil Services Mains exam and appearing at the Interview. I could read their faces right and found that they were curious to hear me. I took advantage of this and started discussing the Geography Syllabus for the Prelims and the Mains exam and the strategy to completely master the whole syllabus within a limited time.

Some students asked –"sir, how many hours a day is good enough for the success in the Civil Services Exam."

Some asked–"sir how many hours did you study everyday"

Some others asked–"how can we score maximum in Geography in minimum time."

I replied–"each one of you is a different

individual with different requirements and needs a different approach, a strategy of your own as I have developed for myself over a period of time. I call it a 'time-target' approach. It means that it's not important how many hours a day you study. What is important is the amount of content you must study over a period of time. You can decide how much time it would take checking your own pace of learning. You should also focus only on the content mentioned in the syllabus of the Civil Services Exam for each subject and the past year question papers for this exam. You can make an intelligent guess from the questions asked in the past and come to a list of the most probable questions that are the most likely to appear in the next year exam. Please also keep an eye over the currents events related to Geography viz. environmental change, volcanic eruptions, earthquakes, tsunamis, population explosion and depletion, discovery of earth's natural resources etc."

They looked satisfied with my answers. I was also satisfied with my performance. My first class was like a meditation session. I had my full concentration while answering their questions. I met the director again. She ordered two cups of coffee. She asked- "how was the class? Would you be able to teach them?

I smiled and said-"yes I would. I have just discovered that I enjoy teaching."

She thanked me for taking the class and said-"I'll talk to the students and give you a call tomorrow."

I thanked her once again for the wonderful opportunity she had given me and returned to my hostel in JNU, quietly ate my dinner in the hostel mess and went out for a post-dinner walk.

The next day I got a call in the afternoon. She said-"Please come prepared in the evening today to teach Geography. You are part of the IDP3 faculty now. Students want you here"

I really needed this job. I was so happy. It was beginning of a success story. It felt great that students wanted me to teach them even though I was younger than most of them. I revised the topic twice before starting off to the coaching institute. After a fifteen minute walk I reached the institute. I told the waiting students in the classroom-"here I am not to teach you but to learn together. I believe that each one of us here has the potential to be better tomorrow than one is today. Let's start learning now."

They all said in one voice-"we'll learn together"

I had developed a very good rapport with them in the first class itself and since then the job was easy. We enjoyed learning together.

The Director of the Institute offered me to give Rupees 15,000 in three instalments for the whole course lasting over three months. I immediately accepted her offer as any money was good for me those days. I had unlimited joy spreading within me that time. I had made a start. I could earn now.

I went for the M.Phil. classes to CSRD and prepared for the Mains exam at the same time. Mains exams were just a month away. I was putting efforts for Psychology and had formed a team to study Psychology with Chetan, a KM College senior, who lived in *Mukherjee Nagar*[9], North Delhi. He had also studied Psychology from the same coaching institute

---

[9]   A place in north Delhi where a large number of Civil Services aspirants live in the rented flats and prepare for the Civil Services Exam

and had the same *Mukul Pathak's*[10] notes. Nevertheless his notes were so well made that I could not stop myself requesting him a photo copy of his notes. Just like a perfect gentleman he gave me his notes with pleasure. I made most out of those notes. Overnight studying Psychology became easier and my major worry got over.

I was ready for the Mains exam now. I could walk properly and even jog. The world felt so good as if some precious lost gift had returned to me. I took a break from the IDP3 to write my mains exam with a promise to come back soon after my Mains exam got over. I and my room mate Avinash had the same examination centre so we hired a cab together in morning and set out for the examination centre. Avinash's girlfriend accompanied him too. On the way she sharpened his pencils and carried apples for lunch. My examination went well. Nothing was difficult or tricky except the statistics part in the General Studies paper. Psychology paper was interesting and it was fun writing it as out of five questions I had

---

[10]   The most successful Psychology coach for Civil Services Exam

guessed three beforehand and had their answers very carefully and had mugged up their answers well just before the Mains exam. Geography papers were interesting too and this time I had revised them well while teaching in the coaching institute. After the exam got over I was back to my students at the coaching institute and also to the CSRD for the M.Phil. classes. Professors at CSRD had been looking for me since many days as I had been absent from the classroom on account of my Mains exam. They knew it already as many other students were absent too for the same reason so they did not ask me many questions about my absence but looked angry with me. I became regular in the class after the Mains exam and made up for most of the lost time studying from the previous notes of my classmates.

In the M.Phil. class there were a few new faces but the large part was the old stock from the M.A. Geography class at CSRD. D. Shravan, a young man from Hyderabad was one among the new faces in the M.Phil. Class. We lived in the same hostel and one day we met in the corridor. He introduced himself and I instantly found a friend in him. Since that day we became bosom buddies. Together we went to the classes, ate lunch, played table-tennis, drank *chai*[11] at the *dhaba* in JNU and went around the JNU campus riding his bike. We went to the stadium for the evening jog everyday. Life once again felt good and I relaxed in his company. After my Mains exam I had a lot of free time and I used this opportunity to read books. I truly enjoyed reading "Glimpses of the World History" by Jawaharlal Nehru and learned a great deal about what happened around the world in last five thousand years. It proved just to be an appetizer. The main course followed after that. I started reading books written on India by various authors. "India an Emerging Power" by Stephan P. Cohen was the book I recommended many of my friends who wanted to understand India better. "The idea of India" by Sunil Khilnani was another good book that I read during that time.

Time flied during those relaxed few months and it was time to face the result again. My Mains exam had gone well and I was almost sure to get a call for the Interview though one

---

[11] Tea

could never be fully sure about the unpredictable results of the Civil Services exam. I did get a call again to appear for the Interview. This time it was on Thursday. Just a few days before the day of the Interview I had read "Ignited Minds" by Dr. A.P.J. Abdul Kalam. It was such an inspiring and strength-giving book that I kept it with me all the time those days. When I went inside the Interview hall where students were waiting for their turn, I kept on reading it. I felt strong and motivated. Rajesh *bhaiya*[12] was also appearing in the interview at the same time and I read him a few paragraphs from the book. It had magical impact on him. He was feeling nervous but soon started feeling positive and confident after I read a paragraph from that book to him. His turn came first so he went in. I waited for another few minutes. My turn came and I entered the room wishing all the members 'good morning'. There were five persons inside. In front of me across the oval table was seated the Chairperson *Mr. A.K. Banerjee*, there were two members sitting on the left and two on the right side of the Chairperson. On my left sat a

---

[12] A term of respect used for someone slightly elder than oneself

lady who later kept watch on my body movements and I rightly guessed she was a Psychologist. They asked me to sit and I thanked them.

The Chairman started-"why did you come from Nalanda to Delhi for getting a graduation degree, why not Patna?"

I replied-"sir, Nalanda does not have a University anymore as it used to have the reputed Nalanda University centuries back and the educational institutions in my state do not finish the courses at time. Exams are delayed, publication of results is also delayed and students lose a lot of time in these circumstances. For example a three year degree course takes more than four years to complete. Besides that even the standards of teaching have gone down. The college campuses are highly politicized and that takes a lot quality time of a student."

He was not very satisfied with my answer and asked me to speak more on it. I could not think of many other things except that-"sir I always wanted to study in Delhi University."

He shifted to my hobby- Transcendental Meditation or TM in short. He asked-"what do you do while you meditate, just go off to sleep?!"

I said-"sir, meditation is an active process, very different from sleep. It's sleep-like but person who meditates is conscious, a train of thought passes through his mind and he does not focus or stop at any one thought. He lets all pass through as the train passes."

He asked-"what is TM?"

I replied-" it's a special form of meditation developed by *Maharishi*[13] Mahesh Yogi which is very easy to practice and can be practiced any time of the day for a duration of fifteen to thirty minutes, at any place even while travelling. A person first repeats a word many times, the word that is very dear to him or a word that means a lot to him. Slowly the person gets lost into a thought process, loses that word and gets lost in the train of thoughts running through his mind. After some time even these thoughts, basically the remains of the day disappear and an absolute calmness descends on the person. The body gets relaxed and peaceful. In the end when the person wants

---

[13] Great saint

to come out of this state he starts increasing his breathing speed. After a while the person returns to his previous state."

He asked-"what happens after that?"

I said-"it's like a mental bath. All the thoughts that clutter ones mind are washed away. Mind feels fresh once again."

He looked satisfied with my answer and moved to another question.

He asked his colleagues on his left to ask me questions. He looked at the information I had filled up in the Mains written form and asked me about debating and my experience in the World Universities Debating Championship in Manila. He asked me to speak for and against any topic of my choice. I chose to speak for and against the removal of Saddam Hussein. He looked satisfied. Then he continued asking- "where did democracy appear for the first time in the world? What kind of system did it follow?

I answered-"the world's first democracy appeared in *Licchavi*[14] Republic that is present day *Vaishali* district in the Indian State of Bihar.

---

[14]   It existed around two millennia back in India

It had *Sabha*[15] and *Samitis*[16] that helped in governing the republic.

Next he asked-"what do you prefer 'democracy without development or development without democracy?"

I said -"for me democracy and freedom is as important as water is for the fish, I can live without development but not without democracy."

He cited the example of China that was growing so fast because it was not a democracy and did not have to deal with many institutional requirements before taking decisions.

I gave the example of India that had so much diversity and yet a functional and developing society because it had chosen democracy.

He did not ask any more questions and looked at the person sitting next to him. He asked -"can you tell me the name of the celebrity who is associated with Transcendental Meditation?"

---

[15] Assembly
[16] Committees

I answered –"yes, Sir Paul Mac Courtney of *Beatles*[17] fame."

He looked happy from my answer and continued asking- "why did you opt for the Indian Foreign Service?"

This question I had prepared well in advance because I was expecting it to come up in my interview. I replied-"India's rising profile in the world demands that this civilization-state pays greater attention to the global issues that affect the future of the whole mankind and I believe that Indian diplomacy can play a vital role in making the whole world a better place to live and as an Indian diplomat I can actively participate in this historical process."

He looked satisfied from my answers and continued asking more questions. He asked-"are democracies perfect and is there any perfect democracy today in the world?"

I said-"no, democracies are not perfect and there is no perfect democracy today in the world. Democracy is not a point but a continuum. Somewhere it reaches, let us say, up to eighty five percent on the continuum

---

[17]   A very famous English rock group

while in other places it is, let us say, below twenty five percent, continuous endeavour should be made in making them more democratic in different parts of the world. It should not be forgotten that every society defines democracy in its own way and each could become more democratic without losing one's own unique qualities. There is no democracy today in the world that does not have the scope of becoming even more democratic."

He looked happy and looked at the lady sitting on my left. She appeared to me a Psychologist since the beginning as she was closely monitoring my body and hand movements since the beginning. She asked me- "please tell me one principle or theory of Psychology that you have applied to your life?"

I replied-"it is *Maslow's*[18] theory of *motivation*[19], though I have not fully applied it to my life, I am in the process of applying it.

---

[18] Abraham Maslow

[19] A theory of human motivation that says that there is a hierarchy in motivation and once our basic needs are met we are motivated by the higher needs like needs of security, belongingness, self-esteem and ultimately Self Actualization

My physiological needs are already met. What I need is 'to belong' and if I join the Indian Foreign Service, even this need would get fulfilled. Then I would give my best each and everyday and may be one day I would achieve 'Self Actualization' as well.

The answer took her and the rest of the members by surprise. I realized only after finishing that it was a master-stroke on my part and the lady on my left did not ask any more questions. She was more than satisfied. Now the last member's turn came. He asked me questions from Geography viz. "what is the length and breadth of India?" He asked a tricky question in the end which I could not answer. The Chairperson said it was a *googly*[20] and answered himself. With that ended my Interview. I felt satisfied and walked back to the waiting room smiling. Many who were waiting there asked me about the Interview and I narrated as it had happened. Soon I got out of the building and came on Shahjehan road and took a deep breath looking back at the high central dome of the *Dholpur house*[21].

---

[20]   An unexpected move, a blind spot
[21]   Place where interviews for the candidates of Civil Services are conducted

I had always been in awe with it. Today I had come out of it feeling triumphant. I took an auto rickshaw and headed towards JNU.

My friend Shravan had come to pick me up from the Shahjehan road after my Interview was over. I found it when I reached the campus as I did not have a cell phone those days. I felt as if I had done some great mistake, I should have waited for him but I had hurried up in getting back to JNU. Anyway he came back and I said sorry to him and then we spent the whole day together talking and strolling, drinking many cups of tea and meeting different people in the campus. They all wanted to hear about my Interview and how had it gone. I narrated the whole sequence many times since that day whenever someone or the other asked me about my Interview. Now I had to start preparing again for the Prelims that was going to take place in less than a month's time. I went for a walk in the evening and jogged in the morning for keeping myself healthy and my stress levels under control. I played table-tennis regularly with Shravan as it was always fun to play this game and waited for the final results.

9

Enchanting Hills of Mussorie

What if you slept?

And what if, in your sleep you dreamed?

And what if, in your dream, you went to
heaven and plucked a flower?

And what if you awoke you had the flower
in your hand?

Ah what then?

- Coleridge

Soon the final results of the Civil Services
exam were out. I was a bit nervous this time

because I had bitten the dust in the end after getting past the Prelims and the Mains exams of the Civil Services. I could not gather up my courage to see the results myself so I requested my friend Soma, who lived in the building just opposite the *UPSC*[1] building on *Shahjehan road*[2], to go across the road and check the results. In the meanwhile someone told me that my roommate Avinash had stood second topper in the Civil Services Exam 2002. I was very happy for him but at the same time my heart had started to beat faster. I too imagined making it to the top. I was eagerly waiting for Soma's phone call. Every moment was passing with great speculation and I was getting impatient. I was hovering around the phone restlessly waiting when it would ring. I waited and waited. Each moment felt like a year. Finally the phone rang after fifteen minutes. She almost cried with joy telling me -"you got the seventy first rank in the final list. You have finally made it. I am so happy...so happy you have made it." She almost broke her ankle while running

---

[1]   Union Public Service Commission- the constitutional body that selects and promotes the Indian Civil Servants

[2]   A road in New Delhi named after the Mogul Emperor Shahjehan who built the famous 'Taj mahal'

back home to give me the news of my success on phone. I was exhilarated, thrilled, my body felt a strange sensation. There were tears in my eyes. I immediately wiped them off and ran to my brother to tell him the good news. I tried to call my parents but could not get through due to the busy telephone line. Shravan was all along with me taking me around on his bike. I went to meet Meghna, my friend and foe since the last three years and my classmate since the College days. We hugged each other for the first time. She was overjoyed and very proud of me as I was her best friend in JNU. My KM College friend and inspiration, Ritika also came to see and congratulate me along with her parents that evening. It was an evening unlike any other evening of my life. I had no hunger, no thirst. My body felt so light. Blood ran faster and the world seemed a different place with me at the centre of it. Truly it was my day. I knew the coming morning would never be the same again. My success was taking time to sink.

I could call my parents only late at night that day. They congratulated me on my grand success. I wished I could immediately fly home to see them; how did they feel, how happy and proud they must be of their son and their decision to move away from the banks of the river Paimar, to save the lives of their little babies, nourish them, educate them! I spent that evening with Shravan and Meghna, my best friends and my elder brother. We went out for dinner to Uddupi; a South Indian restaurant near JNU. My father called me up from home during the dinner that night and advised me to learn a new language in my free time that I was going to have now onwards. Soon I joined the *Alliance Française*[3]. The next morning I woke up early and went out for jogging. I continued teaching in IDP3 even after my success for a few weeks. I spent a lot of time reading books and absorbing the ideas and learning French. I hanged around in the beautiful JNU campus with Meghna and Shravan. We drank a lot of Mango and Papaya shake those days to beat the summer heat. It was the best of the times, glorious and carefree.

It is said that in the success lies the seeds of the failure. Success tasted so good but I knew that the next moment it was going to turn

---

[3]   French cultural center that offers courses in French language

everything upside down. I would soon have to leave the beautiful campus of JNU and the friends whom I loved so dearly, around whom I had spent some of the best moments of my life. 'Success thus comes at a great cost as it came to me.' It was clear to me that I was going to join the Indian Foreign Service, the Service that I had always wanted. It was also true that I was going to travel to different corners of the world leaving my beloved New Delhi but I could not imagine losing my friends who were so dear to me.

Soon I got to know that in the first week of September I would have to join the *Lal Bahadur Shastri*[4] National Academy of Administration (LBSNA) in *Mussorie*[5]. I had less than four months to spend with my friends before I left the beautiful JNU campus. It was time to go home, back to the banks of the river Paimar.

I returned home triumphant and was given hero's welcome at the Rajgir Railway station.

---

[4]   A great leader and India's second Prime Minister after Jawaharlal Nehru

[5]   A picturesque hill station in the central Himalayas where the Indian National Academy of Administration is located. D. Shravan, a young man from Hyderabad

My father came to meet me at the station. I was overjoyed seeing him. His eyes that had bid me farewell one day years ago were welcoming me with such ecstatic joy. We took a *Tumtum*[6] from the Railway station and came to the bus station from where we reached home by a trekker after half an hour's journey. When I reached home, people flocked to see me as if I was a *demigod*[7]. The world had suddenly changed for me. Journalists who reported for the local newspapers came to interview me. The whole village came to see me. They were curious to know if I could help them in getting any government jobs. All my relatives came to congratulate me. They were expecting that they could get some favour or the other from me. It proved to be a difficult time for me. My privacy had gone and I used to be surrounded by someone or the other almost all the time.

My parents were very happy and proud of my achievements. They wanted my elder brother to succeed too. We spent a lot of time together talking about the ways to transform our village. During the last twenty years my

---

[6]   Horse carriage

[7]   Civil servants are still revered in the villages of India as demigods

father had single handily transformed the place of a few hutments into a modern village since the time he had settled there. A small market had appeared over these years and now and it was growing at a fast rate. The length of our village had gone up many times as it continued to grow along both sides of the main road while there was a slight bulge in its width as well, as now the village had spread till the canal. The space on both sides of the road had been taken up by the shops while the interiors were used for building houses. My father had gathered 'a group of the willing telephone subscribers', mainly the new shopkeepers and a few old residents of our village to form a critical mass for getting a telephone connection in the village. They had worked as a pressure group together and pressured the district administration to provide a telephone connection to our village. District administration had agreed in the end for a telephone line to our village after much pulls and pressures. The arrival of telephone line had created a sense of achievement and enthusiasm among the villagers and they had put their case very strongly in front of the district officials and the *Vidhayak*[8] of their constituency for electricity connection to the village. This had brought good results and now the village had electricity connection as well. My father felt very proud of these developments in a small place he had chosen to settle in twenty years back. Why not? He had nursed it carefully for twenty years like his own baby and now it had grown young and beautiful and looked exactly as he had imagined it to be twenty years back. Now he wanted to build a very good school in the village where all the children of the surrounding villages could get good education. He also wanted to build a three bed hospital in the village. We looked for the sites around the village for the school and the hospital when we went for a walk together in the evening everyday like the old times, in the green fields with the setting sun in the background. I used to have transcendental feelings those days walking with my father. Only a painting or a poem can do justice with the feelings and emotions of those times.

Me and my father

Walking on the carpet green

---

[8]   Member of the state legislative assembly

In the open fields
While the Sun set behind
Painting the sky crimson red
Spreading its last rays,
Birds chirping loudly
Flying back home
Cow boys with their cattle
Village girls with grass bundles
All returning home,
Cool Breeze blowing into us
The magic of the moment seeping into soul
Symphony of cicadas
Filling the silence
Transcendental feelings
As if earth meeting the heavens

After a few days of spending time with my parents I went to my birthplace with my father and *Manjhala*[9] *uncle* to see my Grandpa and my other uncles. We tried to reach the village by a trekker but we had to get off from the trekker a kilometre away from my grandpa's

---

9   My father's brother who is the second son of my Grandparents

village. We started walking through the fields as there was no road up to the village even in 2003, the twenty first century. Whole village gathered to see me. We all sat and ate together, took photographs. The old ones told me stories about my childhood days as much as they could remember from their memories. Some of them were pretty embarrassing for me particularly that I never wanted to walk even an inch on my own and always insisted others to carry me either on their backs or shoulders.

My grandpa was a very happy to know about my success. He embraced me while I touched his feet and we conversed for a long time. He was in good health and did not hesitate to prove it to me. He took my right hand into his grip and pressed it hard. I could feel his strength, after all he was a wrestler, though he did not wrestle everyday but the spirit of a wrestler within him had not died. He could still beat a young man like me with his wrestling skills. He taught me some exercises to keep myself fit. In his eighties he was still strong and going while in my early twenties I felt weak at times. Here I had something great to learn from this strong man who had never been away from his village, from the banks of his beloved Paimar, from his birthplace, but he certainly knew the ways of the world far better than I did.

After visiting my Grandpa I went to visit my *nanighar*[10]. My maternal grandpa 'Mahto Ji' and my maternal grandma both had passed away long time back. I met all my cousins, my *mamas*[11] and *mamanis*[12] there as well as the other villagers. We returned home that evening feeling refreshed and rejuvenated.

The next day I was invited to the R.D.H. High School from where I had passed my Matriculation exam in 1994. The Principal and teachers felt proud of my achievements and invited me to high school to welcome and felicitate me. I took this opportunity to say a few words to inspire the students who had come in large numbers to hear me. One of the teachers who had taught me when I was in the high school introduced me to the students. He was my Sanskrit teacher Shri *Jayanandan Pandey* who had inspired me during one of the lowest points of my life around ten years back.

---

[10] Home of the parents of my mother
[11] Brother of my mother
[12] Wife of my mother's brother

I started my speech by saying- "I am one of you. I sat where you sit today and I stood where you stand today. When I was in class tenth, I read a prose titled *Utsah*[13] by *Ramchandra Shukla*[14] in which he said-'*tir ka nishana jitna upar hoga utna hi wo upar jayega*[15]'. This sentence inspired me to aim high and since then I have not looked back.

The other thing I want to share today with you is the story of *Arjuna*[16] and *Dronacharya*[17] from *Mahabharata*[18]. *Dronacharya* asked *Pandavas*[19] to hit in the eye of a bird that was sitting on the tree. He asked *Yudhisthira,* the eldest among the *Pandavas,* to hit first.

Dronacharya asked him-'what do you see *Yudhisthira?*'

He said-'*Acharya*[20], I see the whole tree, the bird and its eye.'

---

[13] Courage
[14] A great writer in 'Hindi' literature
[15] The higher will be the target, the higher the arrow will go
[16] The greatest archer in the epic of Mahabharata
[17] Guru of Arjuna
[18] The greatest Indian epic
[19] Five brothers, Arjuna was one of the Pandavas
[20] Teacher

Dronacharya asked him not to shoot the arrow and called *Bhima*, the second among the *Pandavas*. He now asked Bhima to answer the same question before shooting the bird. He asked the same question from *Nakula* and *Sahdeva* before shooting and all of them replied like *Yudhisthira*. In the end he called *Arjuna*, the best among his disciples and asked him- 'what do you see *Arjuna*?'

Arjuna said-'*Gurudev*[21], I only see the eye of the bird.' *Dronacharya* told *Arjuna*-'then go ahead dear Arjuna and shoot you will definitely succeed in hitting the eye of the bird.' *Arjuna* shot and pierced the eye of the bird.

"The moral of this story is to focus in life on things one wants. 'Focus' is vital in life for the goals one wants to achieve.' My belief is that one can achieve anything in this universe if one really wants it and believes in it. When one tries putting one's heart and mind together, all forces of this universe help him to achieve that goal. So first of all one must know what one really wants and then one should focus on it till one gets it."

---

[21] Reverend teacher

Everyone in the school hall listened to me attentively. It was a great moment in my life to speak to young students full of hope for their future, to motivate them to aim higher, to do better. After my speech the photographs were clicked and sweets were shared. Teachers gave me gifts. After the school function got over a journalist for a regional daily newspaper came for an interview. The next day the newspaper carried a story-

"Determined Nalanda boy succeeds in Indian Foreign Service".

"When there is great willpower, firm determination and a beautiful dream then there is nothing difficult in this world." This is the statement of Shri Kumar who has chosen to serve his country through Indian Foreign Service. He has made his village Chhabilapur and Rajgir very proud by his success in the IFS. He is very happy to achieve his goal and says that one of his dreams has come true and the next one is beginning now. Gifted since childhood he went to Manila, the capital of Philippines to participate in the nineteenth World Universities Debating Championship representing KM College, Delhi University in 1998. His wish is that an

international university should be established in Nalanda district to revive higher education in the State.

In an answer to the question why did he choose Indian Foreign Service as his first choice, he said-"I was born in Nalanda. It's a place which attracts a large number of foreigners from around the world. I have come face to face with them since childhood and learned about various cultures and traditions. I'll like to extend and deepen India's relationship with the rest of the world.'

He said-"he wants to take Indian diplomacy to even greater heights."

"He wants to build a very good school in his village."

After spending fifteen days with my parents at home I was back again to JNU with my friends and with my elder brother. He was in his final year of graduation in the Spanish language three year degree course and was eagerly waiting to join a multinational outsourcing firm after passing out of JNU. He had improved his language skills, both in English and Spanish. Now he could easily converse in English. He had thus overcome a major handicap he had in making a world class career. He had made valuable friends and contacts during his two years stay in and around JNU. A whole new world of the rising outsourcing business had just opened to him as the world was globalizing. India with its vast number of cheap, young and skilled manpower offered the big multinational companies an appropriate place to shift their back office operations by using the latest advances in the internet and data transfer technology. Students passing out from the School of Languages in JNU were in great demand in the call centres of those multinational companies. My elder brother had his eyes firmly fixed on them and the fat salaries they paid.

After spending three more months in JNU, absorbing every ounce of its beauty I moved to the National Academy of Administration *Mussorie*[22] for the seventy fourth foundation course for three and half months. I was touched

---

[22]   Mussorie is a beautiful hill town located in the middle Himalayas around 200km northeast of New Delhi. The Lal Bahadur Shashtri National Academy of Administration is located here where all the Civil Servants begin their careers by attending the Foundation Course.

by the beauty of this lovely hill town as I entered it. The town was founded during the colonial times by the British as a place of rest and recreation from the biting heat of the Indian summer. The old buildings had been preserved well and the streets still had the old classic lamps. Horses were still the best way to go around the town. In short the town still had its old charms intact.

I had come to Mussorie with my classmate from CSRD, JNU Sonam Chombay who had made it to the Indian Revenue Service. He was from Tawang in *Arunachal Pradesh*[23]. According to the rules of the national academy two officers had to share a room in the hostel and no two officers from the same State and from the same Service could live together in the same room. Sonam Chombay and I fitted in this criterion well and we did not loose time in becoming room mates. We were allocated the room number 513 in the Ganga Hostel that was down the slope from the entrance to the Academy. We walked down very carefully with our luggage and got settled in our room. We had not been able to rest even for a while we

---

[23]   One of the seven north-eastern states of India

heard someone knocking the door. 'Chai is ready sir'- the hostel attendant almost barked. As if it was an order rather than a request. We took chai from him and requested him not to disturb us till the afternoon. When we got up in the afternoon we ventured out a little around the campus and immediately found a *dhaba* in the back of our hostel. Our hunger multiplied manifolds after smelling the hot cooking *Alu-Paranthas*[24]. We lost no time in ordering a few delicious *paranthas* for ourselves and since that time we became regular customers of that *dhaba*. We found the 'Happy Valley' soon after and by the evening we had taken a round of the Mussorie mall. For dinner we had to climb up a great distance to reach the Officer's dining hall. That night I met more than two hundred officers in the dining hall. It was the beginning of a new life, life in the Indian Civil Service.

Life at the National Academy of Administration in Mussorie was still a remnant of the days of the *British Raj*[25]. All the officers had to get up early in the morning at five with the ring of a bell and rush to the playground

---

[24]   Delicious pancakes filled with smashed potatoes
[25]   British Colonial Rule in India is often referred to as Raj

called Happy Valley. Mr. Rana, our PT[26] instructor waited for us all there with great eagerness to shape and mould our bodies in his favourite forms. Even a minute's delay invited physical punishment like making several rounds of the Happy Valley, twenty additional push ups etc... Happy valley was such an ironical name. Its right name should have been the 'valley of tears' or the 'Valley of Suffering'. It reminded me of my school days in Rajgir when I had to get up very early in the morning with the ring of the bell and rush to the courtyard for the prayers. I felt as I was back to the school again after passing one of the toughest exams of my life and becoming an officer. The complete lack of freedom to decide about my own life really distressed me. However I soon discovered my love for horse-riding. It was one thing that pleased me a great deal and I found at least something to hang on to while everything else bored me. Besides horse riding, the library and the French classes were interesting. The academy library had a very rich collection of books, magazines, periodicals, journals and newspapers. The video library too

---

[26] Physical Training

had a number of good classics. Each room was equipped with a computer and internet connection. I made very good use of the movie library to watch a number of good classical movies. The dining hall and the class auditoriums were up on the hill while we lived in the valley. Everyday we went up and down many times. The classes used to focus on law, economics and public administration. Only a few out of them were interesting. I particularly liked the law classes by *Mr. Ramchandran*[27]. Those used to be really funny. He started the class by asking every one to clap and giving a riddle to solve so that everybody could pay attention to him. Strangely he used to champion the cause of dowry. We had counsellor groups in which a small number of officer trainees participated and discussed various issues and organized their own food stall during the *Bharat Mela*[28]. Our group put up *'Dosa Hut*[29]*'*. We had a few south Indians in our group and they really knew well how to

---

[27]   A law teacher and a practicing lawyer from the State of Andhra Pradesh

[28]   India Fair

[29]   A food stall that sold Dosai

cook *dosai*[30] and *sambhar vada*[31]. We all got dressed up in south Indian attire with a buttoned shirt and *lungi*[32]. We had a record sale that day and we got a prize for that from the Director of the Academy.

The life at once looked tough as if in a military camp except on every Sunday we were taken to some or the other hill nearby Mussorie for the preparatory training for the grand trekking which was coming a month and half later. Finally we set out for grand trekking in the high Himalayas. It was one of the highest points of my life at the academy. A long distance running race was organized by the Academy towards the end of the foundation course. I did fairly well in that race. I had done well in the horse riding test too and was one of the good horse riders. After all it was the best thing I liked in Mussorie.

I often used to walk on the road from the mall to the Academy after a nice dinner at the Tavern in the weekends. The owner of Tavern

---

[30] A South Indian dish made out of rice flour
[31] Another delicious south Indian dish
[32] More than a meter long one piece unstitched clothe worn around the waist covering the legs in hot tropical climatic conditions

enjoyed singing with his guitar. He sang some
of my favourite songs like 'Nights in white
satin...Country roads take me home... and
many others.' The view of the *Dehradoon*[33] at
night from the terrace of the mall street
enchanted me while I walked back to the
Academy along with friends. *Dehradoon* when
lit up at night looked as if thousands pearls
and diamonds were shining together creating
a cosmic splendour.

My brother visited me at the Academy
towards the end of the foundation course. He
was enchanted by the beauty of the hills of
Mussorie. We walked on the mall road carrying
infectious smiles on our faces. It was a moment
of joy, a moment to cherish as we walked
together into the golden gates of the National
Academy of Administration together. We
walked together with same elegance and sense
of joy when we went to see our grandma and
I held his hand firmly while crossing the river
Paimar. We were together again but this time
we were in the enchanting Himalayas.

---

[33]   A beautiful town in the valley in the Himalayas, capital
of the State of Uttranchal, India

After spending three and half months in the Academy I returned to New Delhi for my further training at the Foreign Service Institute where I spent a year.

10

The Silicon Valley

The bright dawn heralds a new day
Its rosy lances have opened
The golden gates of the Sun
And lit up the path of action
Awake, o man, the slumber
And darkness of the night is over
May each dawn lead us
From triumph to triumph
In the long journey of life

-Rigveda 1.113.16

During this time my brother had already completed graduation in Spanish from the School of Languages, JNU with good grades. Soon he was invited by an outsourcing company in India's Silicon Valley, Bangalore to handle its Spanish and Latin American operations. He worked there for a while but did not really like the working conditions there. The company too lost its contracts because of its unprofessional business practices and some deadline problems. The company got closed and he lost his first job in the outsourcing business. Anyway he wanted to move on and came back to Delhi to spend some time with me and look for a job in the meanwhile. He had learned his lessons and understood the changes which had crept into the job market in the last decade. He had to perform efficiently or he could lose his job. Jobs were not for the life-time anymore. One had to continuously upgrade one's skills and sense the changes in the market trends on the way. It meant continuous evolution and growth of a person.

In Delhi my elder brother used my notebook and internet connection to search for a new job. He did not need to physically go anywhere now to search for a job. Interviews were conducted over the mobile phone. In days time he got a lucrative offer and joined the well-known multinational computer giant *Hewlett Packard* (HP) in *Chennai*[1] as a Contract Administrator for its Latin American Operations. The company sent him an air ticket to fly from Delhi to Chennai, stay in a five star hotel for a month till he made some alternative accommodation arrangements for himself. He started with a fat salary that was four times of my starting salary. My starting salary was not much and I had to wait two years to buy a new car with that kind of salary. My brother soon offered me financial assistance in case I needed to buy a car. This was the journey India had travelled in three generations where the best paid jobs were not the Government jobs but the one in the rising private sector.

Soon he invited parents to visit him in Chennai sending them air tickets, thanks to the low-cost airlines that had started operating in India between major cities. They had never flown in an airplane in their life time thanks to the state monopoly over air travel in the country

---

[1]   A vibrant metropolitan city in South India, capital of Tamilnadu

that kept airfares very high and air travel out of reach of common people for many years. Now the airfares were as low as a first class train ticket. More people could travel from one part of the country to another by air. India was changing slowly and after the entry of my elder brother into the Silicon Valley I felt India had come a long way in the last three generations. It looked a new India to me.

Just fifteen years back me and my brother dreamed to own a new bicycle and we had set a five year plan to save money to buy one. We could not buy a new bicycle even after five years as our savings were not enough and the price of a new bicycle had gone up. But in the last fifteen to twenty years India had undergone a tremendous transformation. The economic reforms of the nineties and the information revolution brought by the mobile revolution in every part of India had transformed the very basics of Indian economy. My parents had never thought even in their wildest imagination that their son would work as a Contract Administrator in a multinational online computer company and would earn a huge salary and perks after learning a foreign language like Spanish and some basic computer skills. Every one thought about becoming a Doctor, Engineer, Bank Clerk, Civil Servant, Lawyer or a Politician but not a Contract Administrator for an online multinational company based in Silicon Valley of India. This surprised me even as the fast changes in information technology had been faster than I used to read in the science fiction stories.

"For me my brother's success is far greater an achievement for me, my family and our country than my success in the Indian Civil Services. He represents a new wave that is sweeping over the globe, the shape of the things to come in the future and the transformation India is going through over the decades."

An ancient civilization is waking up and the whole world is watching India carefully and attentively. Not a single day in the leading or not so leading countries of the world and their capitals passes without someway or the other referring, discussing or quoting India and its economic transformation. The world's fastest growing democracy is at ease with its past and present. It has a large number of its citizens dependent on agriculture while services constitute more than half of its GDP^2. It is surprising but true that India is the world's third largest economy in PPP^3 terms but at the same time shelters millions of poor people living below \$1 a day and almost half of its children are malnourished.

The greatness and beauty of India is in its diversity where past and present live together as my Grandpa and my elder brother coexist side by side. One at ease with grazing cows and growing vegetables in the green fields by the river with his 'river-valley civilization life style' in the 'agricultural age' as he has been there since centuries, since the very beginning of mankind's arrival while the other, my elder brother, in the 'Silicon Valley' at ease with a new era of 'information age' where space and time hardly matter, jobs are available across the globe and business is conducted 24X7 online. Three generations are not a long time in a nation's journey but in this short period of time this is the distance India has travelled.

---

2   Gross Domestic Product
3   Purchasing Power Parity